Alternative Real Estate Research

T0295615

This book aims to provide insight into the 'soft' side of real estate research and the interesting results and implications of real estate research outside the traditional realm of investment/financial aspects. The book also attempts to answer what constitutes the so-called 'soft' side of real estate research if we shift our focus from the usual financial returns and investment analysis. It also attempts to address whether there is such a thing as an alternative real estate research paradigm.

The book also argues that research in real estate should not only be limited to land and property market performance analyses; as this may greatly impair the potential research implications of various real estate studies. The book argues that such analyses take on a very myopic view of real estate research.

This book will interest many who wish to learn more about alternative aspects of real estate research that are more than just about investment analysis.

Ling Hin Li is Associate Professor and the Deputy Head of Department at the Department of Real Estate and Construction of Faculty of Architecture at the University of Hong Kong. He is also the Director of the Surveying BSc Programme and of the China Network MSc Programme at the University of Hong Kong. Ling Hin was Fulbright Scholar in 2005. He was also Visiting Professor at The Institute of East Asian Studies, Lyon, France, in 2004.

Alternative Real Estate Research

Ling Hin Li

with contributions from H. Sun, K. Kwong and T. Chung

Routledge
Taylor & Francis Group

LONDON AND NEW YORK

First published 2015
by Routledge

2 Park Square, Milton Park, Abingdon, Oxfordshire OX14 4RN
711 Third Avenue, New York, NY 10017

Routledge is an imprint of the Taylor & Francis Group, an informa business

First issued in paperback 2018

British Library Cataloguing in Publication Data
A catalogue record for this book is available from the British Library

Library of Congress Cataloging-in-Publication Data
Alternative real estate research / edited by Ling Hin Li.
pages cm
Includes bibliographical references and index.
1. Real estate business. I. Li, Ling-hin, editor of compilation.
HD1375.A538 2014
333.33072—dc23
2014005204

ISBN: 978-1-138-78208-2 (hbk)
ISBN: 978-1-138-31685-0 (pbk)

Typeset in Times New Roman
by Cenveo Publisher Services

This book is dedicated to all Black Sheep in the world

Contents

List of figures

List of photographs and map

Photographs

Map

List of tables

Contributors

Ling Hin Li is Associate Professor and the Deputy Head of Department at the Department of Real Estate and Construction of Faculty of Architecture, University of Hong Kong. He is also the Director of the Surveying BSc Programme and of the China Network MSc Programme at the university. Ling Hin was Fulbright scholar in 2005. He was also Visiting Professor at The Institute of East Asian Studies, Lyon, France in 2004.

Hui Sun currently works at The World Bank in Washington DC, USA. She graduated from The University of Hong Kong in 2009 with a PhD in Real Estate under the supervision of Dr Ling Hin Li. She enjoys yoga and various outdoor activities.

Kevin Ka-ho Kwong graduated from The University of Hong Kong and is a Management Trainee at New World Development Company Limited. He has been awarded the First Prize in The Hong Kong Institute of Surveyors Outstanding Final Year Dissertation Awards 2012.

Tiffany Ka Yan Chung was born in Hong Kong in 1990. She received her BSc in Surveying at the University of Hong Kong, where she developed her insight, critical thinking and analytical skills. Since then, she has entered the construction industry and worked as a Quantity Surveyor in an international consultancy firm.

Acknowledgements

The concept of this book started to emerge in my mind many years ago and I have been pondering how to proceed with it since then. This book could not have been made possible without the help of a number of people. I am very grateful to Mr Tao Siong Lim of Taylor and Francis for his encouragement to send the manuscript to their company for consideration. More importantly, I am indebted to Yongling Lam, Commissioning Editor (Business and Economics) of Routledge, for her unwavering support for this unconventional book idea and daring decision to finally publish it. I am also thankful to Michelle Antrobus and her team at Deer Park Productions for their superb professional work in editing and preparing the final version for publication. I also wish to thank my students, Kevin, Tiffany and Dr Sun for their help in some of the chapters. Last but not least, I am grateful to my family for their support and appreciation.

LH LI
The University of Hong Kong

1 What is real estate research?

L.H. Li

Over the years, the term 'real estate' has been conveniently and automatically associated with 'real estate development' and 'real estate investment' especially in Hong Kong. I cannot resist the temptation of starting this book with two rhetorical questions: 'What is real estate?' and, hence, 'what constitutes real estate research?'. A simple search on the Internet did not yield a direct definition for the phrase 'real estate research'. Similarly, a search in the English-language Wikipedia afforded a response of '*The page "Real estate research" does not exist*', with a large number of suggested sites in the area of real estate economics, real estate investment, real estate development and finance.[1] If there seems to be no definitive boundary for 'real estate research', we will first re-align our attention to just 'real estate'.

According to Wikipedia and the Oxford Online Dictionary, 'real estate' is defined as property that consists of land and buildings.[2] However, most people tend to only associate 'real estate' with investment and monetary return rather than the presence and utilization of the physical structure of land and buildings. This is perhaps due to the fact that in some economies, such as Hong Kong, land and buildings tend to account for a relatively high value figure in the society and consequently also form a more effective vehicle for accumulation of wealth. This also explains why 'real estate research' tends to be investment-biased to the extent that some researchers would only regard research studies accepted by academic journals with a main focus on quantitative investment/financial analyses should be used as a benchmark for measuring different real estate (academic) institutions (Jin and Yu, 2011). Consequently, any research studies pertaining to the analysis of the impact of the use of buildings and land but not directly related to investment or business studies will be regarded as social science studies rather than real estate research. My third rhetorical question in this book therefore becomes, 'does real estate research have to be just about pricing/investment analysis?'

Without an immediate answer for this question, let me point out that real estate as an investment vehicle is quite different from other investment opportunities. Apart from the monetary and financial return, real estate has a much stronger physical presence in society that makes people notice. It is this aspect that most conventional real estate research studies tend to pay less attention to. What I and some of my students would like to argue in this book is that there is also a 'soft' side of real estate research that would also provide the same interesting results and implications as the investment/financial side of real estate research already has. The next issue therefore is, what constitutes the so-called 'soft' side of real estate research if we do not focus on pricing and investment analysis? Eventually, is there such thing as an alternative real estate research paradigm?

Alternative real estate research, as the title implies, is similar to other phrases with the same 'alternative' prefix, such as alternative medicine implies an alternative approach to achieve the same outcome. This outcome in the realm of real estate research is a more comprehensive understanding of how a certain real estate decision or strategy impacts on different aspects or networks of our society. Since real estate is defined as 'buildings and land', real estate decision or strategy therefore also encompasses land use strategies and decisions related to the use of buildings, which leads directly or indirectly to the consequences of the chains of events in these different aspects or networks of our society. Apparently, there are many socio-economic or even political issues that will fall into this category of definition than just business- or investment-related topics.

To delineate or even to revamp the boundary of real estate research is not an easy task, especially when there is a deeply rooted perception in our society in Hong Kong that the mere term 'real estate', or 房地产 in Chinese, has to evolve around the concept of money only. This is especially the case in the recent years of Hong Kong where the whole society has been inundated with an anti-real estate development (or developer) sentiment. Consequently, any term with any hint of association with 'real estate' is almost automatically pigeonholed into the 'business' and 'investment' department. When society starts to project a negative sentiment towards the business and investment sector, people also project the same magnitude of negative sentiment towards 'real estate' since the business/investment sector in Hong Kong is so intertwined with the 'real estate development' sector.

Real estate of course entails the purchasing and selling of land and properties, and hence investment return and analysis from such activities is an important element in real estate research. To conclude that research in real estate should only be limited to land and property market performance analyses is to greatly impair the potential research implications of various real estate studies, not to mention that this is a very myopic view of real estate research. The question is, are real estate decisions solely business decisions, in that only a business view can help decipher a more rational approach in making such decisions?

Real estate decisions do not just impact on the business community or financial consequences as real estate decisions include two sets of outcomes. First of all, there will be financial and business outcomes as real estate activities involve monetary transaction, and real estate assets are probably one of the few commodities that will have an increased value even though they have been utilized and occupied before. However, even in the case of real estate investment trusts (REITs) where trading of the investment is based on share prices, some forms of built structure would be involved that also determines the performance of this investment. As such, there is always a saying in the market that real estate investment is in fact buying bricks and mortar. This contrasts distinctively with other forms of investment which can be purely paper-based or even in electronic format. This leads to the second type of real estate decision outcome, namely built structure of various scales. This built structure represents part of the physical framework of our society that will eventually impact on how we carry out our daily activities in all other aspects within this physical envelope, including of course business activities.

Even in the simplest form of real estate decision, such as a family purchasing a new flat, it would trigger a set of consequences including the financial burden pertaining to this purchase, as well as adjustment of the family members to the new physical environment surrounding the new home. Consequently, family members may have to adjust to the new home-to-work or home-to-school commuting routes, new neighbours as well as new community culture. These new adjustments all originate from that real estate decision at the very beginning. If real estate is simply regarded as part of business studies, then the role of real estate research as a multi-disciplinary academic research field will be greatly diminished. This again feeds into the vicious cycle that real estate will be forever associated with investment and business analyses in the eyes of the general public as well as in the academic world, and the latent impact of this research field in our society will not be fully explored.

I have had numerous experiences of facing dubious looks from the other side of the table when elaborating this belief to people that there is an alternative set of real estate research studies that go beyond mere business and investment analyses. Senior members in the university have questioned the rationale for staff, such as myself, with a background in real estate to wander into this 'alternative' side of real estate research topic areas. Such experiences range from research grant application to a description of research profiles in internal promotion exercises. To me, real estate research sits comfortably as a bridge linking the quantitative and numerical side of investment and economic research to the relatively social and qualitative side of social science research (as depicted in Figure 1.1 on page 4). Real estate research should therefore be regarded as the overlapped area between the two subsets of academic research fields, namely social science research and economic research.

I have also been cast with dubious looks when I tried to explain that a researcher with a traditional education in real estate, and professional experience in general practice surveying (again, such as myself!) should not be barred from attempting to apply his or her knowledge in the real estate market or real estate research to explain other aspects in society that may not be 'real-estate related' in the conventional sense. After all, most of the human activities in the urban environment take place within a certain real estate environment one way or another. Educational research, for example, cannot avoid the issue of school location and neighbourhood land use planning, which is to a certain extent a consequence of some real estate decisions. Urban studies cannot distance itself from understanding how land and the housing markets work. If researchers are to be confined to a narrowly defined research field and not encouraged to explore

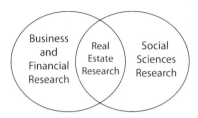

Figure 1.1 Positioning of real estate research.

the potential application of their own expertise in other possible frontiers, a lot of ground-breaking work might not have happened in the academic world. I wish to quote Professor Clive Granger in his Nobel Lecture in Economics acceptance speech in December 2003 to illustrate this point. While explaining his important work in the field of cointegration, he said,

> Before considering the usefulness of the new methods of analysis, I would like to take a personal detour... Previously in my career, I have been Chair of two economics departments, yet I have received very little formal training in economics...Whatever other knowledge I have, it has come from living amongst economists for about forty years, by osmosis, attending seminars, having discussions with them, and general reading. My question is: does this say something about me, or something about the field of economics? I think it is true to say that I am not the first Nobel Prize Winner in economics to have little formal training in economics... Economics does have a multitude of different aspects, applications, and viewpoints which has to each for their own basis, at least in practice... (pp. 363–4).[3]

It would be grossly pretentious of me to try to compare myself with a Nobel laureate, but I find a lot of truth in Prof. Granger's interesting statement and wish to elaborate in this book that it is highly possible to examine various socio-economic issues from a real estate research angle, even though I was not formally trained as a sociologist or social scientist. There is indeed an alternative aspect of real estate research than just investment analysis.

I have asked my student to help me on a very quick search of our online library to see if there has been any research done into crossing real estate and other academic disciplines. Interestingly enough, he found a number of multi-disciplinary studies, including (but not limited to) such areas as real estate and green building (Wedding, 2008; Aroul, 2009); real estate and tree protection (Gerstle, 2008); real estate and nuclear waste transportation (Conway, 2004); and real estate and IT revolution (Dickson, 2002). Again, it seems that real estate forms a good basis for an understanding of various social issues that are not at all related to financial or business analyses, but have an angle in the utilization of land and buildings.

Real estate market – what is it?

I usually start my first lecture in the first year programme with a simple question: 'What is the real estate market, and where is it?' In essence, what do we see in the real estate market? Is it purely a group of businessmen or investors trying to maximize their profit through buying, selling and renting, similar to the famous board game 'Monopoly'? If this is the case, of course, real estate market warrants attention from merely the fields of business, economics and investment, in a way that other financial assets such as the stock market would. But we know that a lot of concerns in the real estate market are not just about whether it is making adequate investment return, but rather whether real estate is affordable. While no one would advocate the government make the share price of some listed companies in the stock market or the price of gold more affordable to the general public, similar demand has been made in the real estate market. In recent years, the phrase 'stabilizing property market' has become an integral part of the political slogan adopted by our government to deal with the runaway housing market in Hong Kong. Slogan aside, can the property market be stabilized and what are the consequences of stabilizing the property market?

In the period between early 1996 to September 1997, the general property price in Hong Kong took a quantum jump of 64.9 per cent,[4] and at the same time, the average number of monthly transactions within this period was 13,810. This came to a peak in April 1997, when it exceeded 23,000 transactions in that month. Two years later, the market collapsed at an unprecedented rate when average residential price level plummeted by 45 per cent by the end of 1999 compared to September 1997. Transaction volume shrank to an average of 8,400 per month, with the lowest point in February 1998, when it just hit slightly above 4,200. This pattern of low-property-price–low-transaction-volume and high-property-price–high-transaction-volume repeated itself during the 2003 SARS epidemic and when hot money flew in during the recovery from the financial tsunami in early 2009.

What do these figures tell us? They tell us that basic consumer behaviour in the property market (as well as investment market in general) is quite different from the expected rational behaviour in any other consumer product markets. In most markets selling consumer durables, such as clothing, toys or mobile phones, consumers defer purchasing when faced with price increases. When taxi fares increase, more people take buses or the underground railway. On the other hand, when price drops, they tend to buy more. This is a rational behaviour generally predicted under the laws of demand and supply. In the real estate market, things work differently because consumers sometimes behave differently or even irrationally. In this market, consumers make a purchase decision on two aspects. There is a consumption requirement (namely for immediate occupation) similar to other products, and there is a long-term investment purpose that is dependent on future re-sale value and cash income flow in between. To make it more complicated, sometimes, it can be both. Consequently, demand factor is more volatile in the housing market compared to commodities, or even other investment products. Therefore, the government will not face that kind of social pressure for action and response if the stock market index in Hong Kong, the Hang Seng Index, soars to more than 35,000 points (at the time of writing, it is around 22,000 points). One would therefore ask what is the government supposed to do when property prices rise too swiftly and by too much? To answer that, one needs to answer another question: What do people want from government action in the housing market?

Homeownership is different from just accommodation, although a direct and core reason for homeownership is to achieve a decent level of accommodation. While accommodation needs cannot be satisfied in a deferred manner, homeownership needs can be. In other words, people do not need to be a homeowner in order to be housed. Renting is always an option as far as finding an accommodation is concerned. However, renting is not normally preferred because, to most people, rental payment is a cost and cannot be re-captured at the end of the accommodation period, unlike mortgage payment. Based on this concept, most people would regard that renting is like helping other property owners to accumulate wealth in real estate. If this is the case then why are there still renters in the housing market? Some may argue that people working in a foreign place would definitely rent rather than buy. Does that mean most local people prefer to buy in their own hometown/city?

According to the study of Bourassa and Hoesli (2010), homeownership rate in Switzerland is only 34 per cent, the lowest in Europe, and very low compared to some Asian cities, including Hong Kong. Even these two scholars note that this seems to be too low, given the relatively affluent status of Switzerland. What is more interesting in their study is that they note that surveys in the country do indicate that most people prefer to be homeowners rather than renters (Bourassa and Hoesli, 2010: 287), but the reality shows otherwise. So what has occurred to change the Swiss' mind? From an analysis of the user cost perspective, they find that there are several reasons contributing to this phenomenon. These reasons include high housing prices for a long time, high property tax and high initial cost (20 per cent down payment) for owning, while there is substantial protection for tenants in terms of security of tenure as well as rent increase. From this analysis, the research team also finds that cities possessing similar characteristics also exhibit a low ownership rate, such as San Francisco (estimated to be 35 per cent) in America (versus a national average of 66 per cent, Bourassa and Hoesli, 2010: 307). So it is true that high property prices work as a detriment to homeownership! If we follow this logic, it will seem to make sense that for any government advocating higher homeownership, the first task is to make sure that property price level remains low. In fact, this observation follows exactly what basic economic principles predict – that when prices go up, demand shrinks. Hence, rising or high property prices (moving from P2 to P1 in Figure 1.2) serve as a deterring signal to fence off additional housing demand (dropping from Q2 to Q1), and vice versa.

However, if we examine these reasons, we find that Hong Kong actually fits into a category of property market where high housing prices together with high entry cost (30 per cent down payment) coexist, although we no longer have a tight tenant-protection mechanism in the Landlord and Tenant Ordinance. But in contrast to this pattern, we have a relatively high homeownership rate. So in our

Figure 1.2 Basic demand and supply interaction.

market, high property prices do not deter people from being homeowners. On the contrary, rising prices encourage people to purchase more. Is the Hong Kong housing market abnormal? Or are the players in the Hong Kong housing market behaving very differently from other markets?

There is indeed nothing wrong with the property market in Hong Kong. Apparently, the 'pull' factors of rising property prices outweigh the issue of affordability, especially in the pre-1997 market era when everybody still held the belief that property prices would only go up. These pull factors work as a reinforcement to boost market players' belief that rising property prices are a signal for entering the market, because the re-sale value is going to be much higher than the purchase price. So what has conditioned the mind of the players in the market such that they tend to demand more when prices are up?

If we look back at the history of Hong Kong's property market, we find that in the period between 1982 and mid-1997, our housing market had been on a steady rise. What is more interesting is the fact though there were some setbacks in the market during this period; every time the market retreated from the peak due to various reasons, the bottom level always stayed higher than the previous bottom. On the other hand, when recovery came, the next peak always arrived at a higher level than the preceding peak in the cycle, until this pattern was broken after 1997 (Figure 1.3). With this market reinforcement of the perception of ever-lasting rising property prices, there seemed to be no question of 'when' in most people's mind when considering buying a flat.

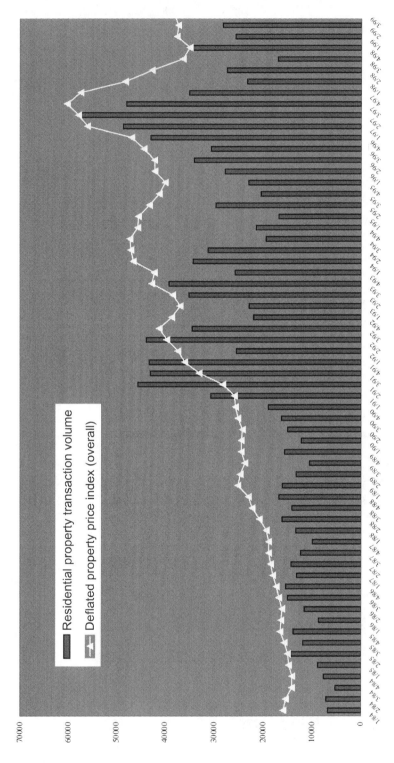

Figure 1.3 Transaction volume and property price levels.

This reinforcement in fact came from more than psychological or irrational judgement. Since the establishment of the currency peg with the US dollar, the Hong Kong government has been deprived of one monetary tool to deal with inflation, namely interest rate adjustment. We can look back in our history and find that inflation in Hong Kong in the pre-1997 era had been rampaging while the market interest rate had not been able to suppress that trend. Given that the overall investment market in Hong Kong, especially in the pre-1997 era, had been dominated by the property sector either in direct property investment or indirect property investment, namely shares of the property-related companies listed in the Hong Kong Stock Exchange, it is no surprise that most people in Hong Kong had drawn their conclusion that investment and 'real estate' were interchangeable terms.

As such, one would see that, in actual fact, the housing market in Hong Kong, unlike the stock market or a fish market, is basically 'everywhere'! Once someone becomes the legal owner of a real estate, he/she becomes also part of the housing supply mechanism, and hence part of the market. It becomes unnecessary to judge whether this owner is holding on to the property for owner-occupation or investment, because, at the end of the day, when the price is right and other conditions are fulfilled, this owner is going to sell. That means most (if not all) owner-occupiers will one day sell their flats, most likely for monetary or other reasons. The reality is, if the owner is not under duress to sell, monetary gain is a major factor for consideration. At this point, is this capital gain so different in nature from an investment gain made by a property investor? In this respect, is it even possible for the government to devise a housing policy that will have differential treatments on the owner-occupiers and the 'investors' respectively?

The fact is, every homeowner, be they owner-occupier or investor, desires to see the property market going up and everybody desires to see that the point he/she enters the market is the lowest possible point before it moves upwards, even where there is no immediate intention to sell. In Hong Kong, we have a saying that the government should clamp down the high housing price level so as to allow people to 'get on the bus'. However, what goes without saying in this request is, once people are on the bus, they all want the bus to start the engine and move. This means most homeowners do not really want to see housing prices being 'stabilized' and would expect their house value starts to grow with the economy or they may consider deferring the purchase decision for the simple logic of opportunity cost, other things being equal (I will explore this later). On the other hand, there are always potential 'prospective homeowners' coming to the market looking for flats, noticeably the younger generation who have just graduated and started their career, and new immigrants. Consequently, 'getting on the bus' is a never-ending request that will recur almost every few years.

Since this lowest possible point is difficult to ascertain and given that most people are risk-averse, most people will execute this decision to purchase when they are really sure that the market trend is on the upward movement. When there are enough people in the market behaving like this, aggregate demand will increase which may lead to increase in price level. By this time, it then almost becomes a self-fulfilling prophecy that property prices will rise once they have entered the market. From this, we can see that rising market price is a reinforcement people seek when they are considering the purchase option. If this pattern is consistent enough over a period of time, such as during the period 1982–1997 in Hong Kong, it is therefore natural for people to consider buying a flat when they witness a rising trend, while probably postponing this option when they see otherwise.

In recent years, there has been a popular saying referring to the skyrocketing housing price phenomenon that 'the price of flour is higher than the price of bread'. Can or should any government try to control land and housing prices in order to make the price of 'bread' more affordable by most people in society? We can examine an interesting policy direction issued by the Australian government in the 1970s.[5] In this report, a number of urban land problems were examined and analysed. In particular, the report highlighted the problem of high land price and commented that '...if the price of land is high, it might encourage development at densities that are too high... many people who would prefer to live in a house at low to medium density are forced to live in flats, partly because of the high price of land...'. Accordingly, a solution to this problem is to exert land price control. It is easy to understand this apparent logic of price control as a means of improving housing affordability. Most people think high property/land price is the cause of all problems in the housing market. Hence, for any government who can suppress the housing and land prices, they will help people to become property owners by doing so.

This is an interesting angle as similar arguments in the social or political context have been made against real estate development in various cities' urban centre for a long time. This argument assumes that land prices rise exogenously and independently from the existing demand trend in the real estate market.

In reality, however, the logic works in a reverse direction. This implies that it is the increase of demand of people to live in the city centre that is the cause for the rise in housing prices that in turn fuels the rise in land price in such location. Higher housing prices, everything being equal, would contribute to higher land prices. Developers who purchase land at the higher price level would therefore need to develop intensively in order to be able to recoup the high development cost. Hence, a highly intensified and developed city centre is a response and solution to higher market demand for using such prime locations. What the report above states that higher development intensity in city centres deprives people from the choice of having a low-density development lifestyle is not sound logic, but rather an acceptable political argument that most people in the society will readily accept.

If we do put a cap on land price with a hope of stopping development intensity, or to lower housing prices, one of the following two things will happen: first of all, if capping land prices in prime locations does not entail capping housing prices on the same locations at the same time, there is no guarantee that controlling land prices would automatically create an affordable housing price level. This is true even when the developers initially price their housing projects according to the low development land cost. Once the affordable cheap housing units have been put to the market due to the low land cost, market demand for such cheap and affordable housing units are going to drive up the price level due to high competition among prospective buyers and, eventually, these units will become expensive. On the other hand, if there is a parallel price cap on the housing prices on these locations, then there is a problem of rationing these affordable housing units. The issue becomes who should be allowed to purchase these cheap units and why. Should it be based on needs or just a lottery as in the case of the subsidized housing programme, the Home Ownership Scheme (HOS), in Hong Kong? In any case, one cannot see that controlling land price will actually solve the problems depicted in the Australian government report mentioned above, that a freedom of choice to live in a low-density environment in the city centre is being granted to the people.

In a recent open forum organized by the government of Hong Kong on public housing subsidies, some younger members of the audience openly called for the development of 'Youth Housing'. This raises the alarm of growing dissatisfaction among the younger generation in their housing needs and their desire to have public housing as their safety net. Young people (say in the 25–34 age group) face a lot of important decisions because they are in transition between different life stages and because they are constrained by many factors while facing a lot of variables. One such important decision is homeownership and housing tenure choice. In fact, in that forum mentioned above, a university student told the government official attending the forum that his girlfriend told him that she would not marry him if he could not be a homeowner! This brings us to a very interesting question: how much should the government do to help housing of the younger generation? Should the government also keep the market entry threshold low in order to stimulate affordable homeownership? If so, how? I explored this 'getting on the bus' argument above. I will elaborate a bit more here.

In recent years, due to runaway housing prices in the private sector of Hong Kong, the younger generation in this city have found it more and more difficult to be homeowners. There is a growing belief from the younger generation that the government has a duty to house them or to provide affordable housing for them. Housing the younger generation in Hong Kong has become such a topical social issue amidst the current anti-developer sentiment in the city that some property tycoons even have to make a friendly gesture to this issue.[6] At the same time, there is also a growing tendency for young people and even university graduates to apply for public housing (single-person units) as soon as they reach the age of 18, when they are legally eligible to apply. Hence, the concern of the young people in both the private and public channels of housing supply for their housing demand to be met is snowballing with the apparent ever-increasing housing price levels in the city.

I did a questionnaire survey with a group of young people (about 620) in the 25–34 age group in early 2013. These respondents were all renters and all had a full-time job at that time. The research was basically about examining the factors affecting their decision to purchase a residential flat in Hong Kong. However, as a side dish, I included an extremely hypothetical question at the end of the questionnaire: '*Would you consider buying a residential flat in Hong Kong now if the government announces an extreme administrative measure to freeze all housing prices in Hong Kong back to the 2005 level with immediate effect, assuming that this measure could not be revoked by any subsequent government action in the future?*' Of course, this is purely hypothetical. The intention of this extreme situation is to examine how people feel if the housing market can be constantly 'stabilized', which has been a major request by most of the people in this city who cannot find an affordable housing. The hypothetical situation is set back to the year 2005 when the housing market in Hong Kong just recovered from the unprecedented catastrophe left behind by the SARS epidemic. A lot of people today are still joking, with regret, 'if only I had purchased a house back then…!' to reflect their nostalgia of the time when housing units were still affordable. Hence, this extreme policy variable asks the respondents whether they would consider buying a residential flat if an extreme government form of intervention were to be put in place to push the clock back to the year 2005 and to freeze the housing price level at the point *forever*. This variable aims at examining whether homebuyers want to see housing prices being kept constant forever, or they just wish to see low housing price before they purchase so as to allow them to get on the bus, but not after! Our survey results show that the policy has the least appeal to wealthier respondents with children who are renters in the private sector. It tends to have a greater positive impact among lower-income females or families currently renting public housing. It therefore illustrates that most potential homebuyers do not wish to see the market being stagnant after they have become a homeowner for the simplest reason of high opportunity cost. Housing units remain an important wealth accumulation tool for most families, even though they did not purchase the flats entirely for investment purposes at the beginning. Government intervention in the housing market therefore is not justified if the objective is merely to artificially lower the market price level. A price-oriented intervention approach would not stimulate more homeownership and would certainly not satisfy housing demand.

From this brief discussion, I hope to point out that understanding what real estate is about and how a real estate market operates is a pre-requisite for a more complete realization of what real estate research entails. This book is based on some studies and issues evolving around the real estate market in Hong Kong. While this may be too localized for some readers, I think the importance of the core issues remains. Besides, one cannot illustrate essence of knowledge if one cannot tell the story with what is going on in his/her own environment. More importantly, Hong Kong is one of the very few real estate markets which are operating within a free market economy and very active, and where the government actually owns the legal title of all land as if it were a socialist economy! By using Hong Kong as an example, I will be elaborating on the possible research topics from my own work and joint work with my students as an illustration to show that there is indeed a very wider spectrum of opportunities to relate some social and non-investment-oriented issues from a real estate perspective when we do not confine ourselves to define 'real estate' as only about business and investment studies. The technical details of these studies will not be elaborated in the chapters, as the objective of this book is to advocate a wider definition of real estate research, not to explore technicalities.

Notes

1 For example, <http://en.wikipedia.org/w/index.php?search=real+estate+research&button= &title=Special%3ASearch>.
2 http://en.wikipedia.org/wiki/Real_estate
3 Source: MLA style: 'Prize Lectures in Economic Sciences 2001-2005'. Online. Available: <http://www.nobelprize.org/nobel_organizations/nobelfoundation/publications/lectures/ WSC/econ-01-05.html> (accessed 16 July 2012).
4 Source: <http://www.rvd.gov.hk/en/publications/pro-review.htm>.
5 Department of Urban and Regional Development, Australian Government (1974) *Urban Land: problems and policies*.
6 http://www.scmp.com/news/hong-kong/article/1254280/henderson-chief-give-land-flats

2 Welfare housing – friends or foes?

L.H. Li and Kevin Kwong

Welfare housing, whether in the form of rental housing or homeownership, such as the subsidized housing programme in Hong Kong, the Home Ownership Scheme (HOS), has always been a topical issue in the academic world. In Hong Kong, developers and private homeowners paid very little attention to the welfare housing sector before 1997, even though approximately half of the population lives in welfare housing in the city. After 1997, welfare housing suddenly became a very controversial issue, especially the HOS projects. Developers and private homeowners blamed HOS projects for dragging down the property price level between 1998 to 2003. On the other hand, most people tend to agree that welfare rental housing should be retained or even expanded as this is part of the welfare safety net. What we find interesting is that while some political parties in Hong Kong support this notion of expanding public rental housing and resurrecting the HOS scheme after it was suspended in 2002 by the Hong Kong government due to various reasons, these very same political parties also object to the government's plan to build public rental housing near the private housing community! We therefore cannot help but think: What damage can public housing do to our private housing market? In this chapter, we hope to unfold this mystery by examining whether and how public housing impacts on the neighbouring private housing community.

Introduction

Not in my back yard (NIMBY) is a term coined to refer to all 'perceived' undesirable effects that are brought to our neighbourhood by, mostly, some government actions and policies, irrespective of the nature of the policy/action itself. Typical examples are medical centres for highly contagious or social diseases, or for the mentally impaired, built next to a housing community. The negative impacts may be real measurable damages or mainly 'perceived' effects with really no experimental or empirical proof of physical damage by the mere existence of such facilities. However, the psychological effects and the repercussions on the market and the society are usually large enough for political groups to cash in. In the field of housing studies, there is a similar argument about the effect of mixing different housing communities/household groups together. Again, there is no consensus on the direction and magnitude of the impact. A major reason for this problem originates from the lack of a definitive measurement of 'back yard' in NIMBY. It is difficult to define a 'comfortable' distance for residents in a certain housing community to accept the existence of 'less desirable neighbours'. This degree of visibility becomes more acute when we study such impact in a compact and highly developed metropolitan city, such as Hong Kong. In Hong Kong, it is interesting to notice that it is not unusual for a number of middle-/high-class residential communities to neighbour with public housing estates, yet we have seen the most dramatic price upsurge in this market during the 1990s. Moreover, this is a mature city with no racial tensions so that the study of impact of public housing on the private housing market can concentrate on the effect of proximity to the welfare housing. Li (2005) conducts an empirical research, which shows that public rental housing in Hong Kong did pose as a suppressive factor in the price level of the neighbouring private housing market. However, this impact is more likely to be psychological. In the following, an extension of this study will be illustrated by further unfolding the story, first looking at some empirical analyses of whether and how public housing may pose as a threat to the private housing community nearby and we will then explore the reasons behind it.

Impact of public/subsidized housing on the neighbourhood

Public housing has been infamously associated with the ghetto almost all around the world.[1] There are many reasons for this connection, not least the social and economic status of the households living in public housing. Public housing is regarded as a social welfare package in most societies and therefore only those families that barely can make ends meet will opt to live there. Because of such a negative 'conglomeration' effect, people living there, especially young people, will be deprived of the opportunity to expand their social network, to acquire new knowledge and to gain access to better job opportunities. Freeman and Botein (2002) outline four major aspects on which public/subsidized housing would have an impact. They are: property values in the neighbouring private housing communities; racial transition; increased concentration of poverty, or the negative conglomeration effect described above; and finally increased crime rate. Since this chapter looks at the effect on property values, we will concentrate on this aspect.

In many societies around the world, public housing has long been positioned as a social welfare package, especially for low-income families that can hardly make a decent living. Because of the economically and socially deprived status of the households in the public housing estates, publicly subsidized housing projects have also been regarded as underprivileged minority groups' last resort of accommodation arrangement.

Due to such an intrinsically negative image of public housing, many people always associate various social issues with public housing estates. Previous literature conclude that people often link a range of social issues to public housing development projects, including property value, racial transition, crime and poverty concentration.

In the US, more and more cities have become home to a growing concentration of poor households disproportionately composed of racial and ethnic minorities. The high concentrations of underprivileged people in those central cities are especially prevalent in each country's social housing or publicly subsidized housing estates. Carter *et al.* (1997) examine the effect of public housing on neighbourhood poverty rates in some cities in the US by constructing a longitudinal database from 1950 to 1990 for four modern cities: Philadelphia, Detroit, Cleveland and Boston. They also investigate the relationship between the locations of public housing projects and changes in neighbourhood poverty rates. They conclude that the relationship between public housing and changes in neighbourhood poverty is both positive and statistically significant as well. The research study, hence, suggests that the public interventions by the government in the housing market, ostensibly designed to help the poor households and their neighbouring communities, may actually and unintentionally exert an opposite impact on them.

In addition to the poverty concentration problem, people might also usually link public housing to crime. For this reason, Farley (1982) examines the patterns of crime in and around public housing developments in the US. In this study, data were gathered from the police on the incidence of crime in multi-block areas consisting of 10 public housing estates in St. Louis from 1971 to 1977. There is a mix of low-rise and high-rise developments, as well as conventionally and tenant-managed housing development projects. Crime rates per 100,000 population were computed for the sake of this study. The research results indicate that the crime rates per 100,000 population in and also near the public housing estates are not significantly higher than in the city as a whole, in particular for those more serious crimes such as arson, murder and drug-trafficking. In addition, there is no concrete evidence supporting the myth that the crime rates are overall higher than the average figures in smaller or larger publicly subsidized housing development projects.

On the other hand, it has been consistently argued that people who live in public housing, particularly teenagers, are of low self-esteem and are often deprived of the opportunities to expand their social networks owing to the adverse image of public housing estates. Even though it is widely assumed that public housing projects are not good for children, there is little empirical research to support this argument.

Currie and Yelowitz (2000) combine information from several sources in order to take a look at the effect of public housing projects on educational attainment. In the view of the adverse image of publicly subsidized housing developments, their results are surprising. While the correlation between public housing projects and the kids' education outcome is negative, they conclude that this is probably due to the unmeasured characteristics of the project participants. As a matter of fact, when these characteristics are controlled, their point estimates suggest that public housing estates may have positive effects on children's academic achievement!

Apart from that, Freeman and Botein (2002) also evaluate the overall neighbourhood impacts resulting from the publicly subsidized housing projects. A relationship between the presence of public housing and both property values and crime with both positive and negative effects is established by their research study. Furthermore, they suggest that racial transition is not directly due to the existence of public housing and conclude that whether public housing estates exert any negative effects on poverty concentration has not yet been reached.

Unlike proximity to landfill, industrial buildings or construction sites, in which it is relatively not difficult to recognize detrimental environmental problems ranging from air pollution to noise pollution, the mere proximity to public housing projects does not exert any tangible and direct physical harm to the surrounding neighbourhood. For this reason, the adverse impact on surrounding property price levels related to proximity to public housing developments might actually be psychological rather than physical, where the factors are not indeed easily identified, except of course the potential crime rate, which from the literature above is not conclusive.

There has been little systematic research to reject or confirm whether locating a public housing development project in a neighbourhood would dampen the value of a residential property. Rabiega *et al.* (1984) attempt to address this issue by looking at the property price impacts of two kinds of public housing development projects, including both medium-rise estates for the elderly and small low-rise family estates in low-density and moderate-density neighbourhood areas in Portland. Surprisingly, they conclude that domestic properties gain in value after public housing development projects have been completed in the case of Portland. However, studies which are similar to this one should be carried out in other regions with comparable sizes and dispersion policies in order for the results to be further generalized and applied to other cities.

Indeed, various research studies and empirical analyses have been done previously to examine the correlation between the existence or even proximity of public housing estates and the neighbouring private property prices within the same community. No concrete evidences have been found to prove the existence of any direct correlations (DeSalvo, 1974 and Nourse, 1963).

In addition, MaRous (1996) conducts a market analysis of four very low-income family public housing developments in four growing suburban market areas in Chicago respectively. The evidence and study results indicate that subsidized housing does not necessarily exert any dampening effects to lower the value of neighbouring residential property or further curb the successful market development in the immediate private housing neighbourhood. Good community planning, good design and buffering of the sites as well as good property management are indeed the key factors for neutralizing effects despite public opinion to the contrary.

However, this relationship might not necessarily hold when the residential property market becomes very active. Proximity to dispersed public housing sites within the same neighbourhood could result in a relatively slower growth in housing sale prices in an otherwise booming housing market. There might actually exist a maximum threshold of the publicly subsidized households beyond which such a negative influence is triggered, irrespective of the distance or characteristics of the publicly subsidized housing or occupants (Santiago *et al.*, 2001), but more data are needed to estimate this threshold.

We therefore notice that, even though there are various previous literatures studying the effect of subsidized housing on the adjacent private domestic property values, there is still no consensus on the existence and direction of the impact. The following is our attempt to contribute to this discussion with empirical data from Hong Kong in the recent decade.

Real estate research and public housing in Hong Kong

Li (2005) has shown that, statistically, most home purchasers in Hong Kong put a negative factor on the value of properties which have a neighbouring subsidized housing project when choosing between different private housing projects in a certain district. This negative effect however seems to be neutralized within the same private housing community, as there is no difference between the housing units which are closer to or farther away from the public housing project that sits next to that private housing community. In other words, flats in a certain private housing development that are farther away from a neighbouring public housing project do not enjoy a premium in price over flats in the same development which are directly next to this public housing project, and vice versa. The negative factor seems to be more psychological than physical. For example, one would normally find housing flats which are nearer to such undesirable facilities as a refuse collection centre to be relatively cheaper than those residential flats which are farther away or even shielded from this collection centre by other residential blocks in the same development. The physical damage of air pollution is obvious in this case and will usually be factored in the price according to the distance to this undesirable facility.

In this chapter, we will explain our analysis in examining the relationship between public housing estates and private residential property market to further support the study of Li (2005). In this analytical model, a total of eight popular private housing development projects, including four in Kowloon and four in the New Territory, have been selected in Hong Kong. Particularly, half of them have adjacent public housing estates while the remaining half does not. These latter four communities serve as a control mechanism for comparison purposes. Housing transaction data of the selected private residential properties are restricted to the time period from 1 November 2000 to 31 October 2010 for 10 years. The key reasons behind limiting the time period under investigation are threefold. First of all, during this period, the local private housing market experienced both substantial growth and rapid depreciation. This allows the model to investigate more accurately the correlation.

In addition, another rationale for selecting the aforementioned time period of study is that this period is relatively recent, so that a more updated reference could be reflected. There is still one more significant reason behind this choice. In the last few years, the private domestic property market in Hong Kong has almost fully recovered from the 1997 financial turmoil and the SARS outbreak in 2003. All of the housing price figures and various property price indices point to the fact that the residential property market has peaked at a very high level where ordinary local citizens could hardly afford to purchase a decent flat even in the remote areas of Hong Kong. The runaway property market eventually drew protests from the society and led to the government's attempt to curb the unusual speculations. On 19 November 2010, the Financial Secretary announced that the Stamp Duty Ordinance would be amended so as to introduce a Special Stamp Duty (SSD) payable upon disposal of residential properties on top of the currently implemented ad valorem property transaction stamp duty. Under such a new policy, any residential properties acquired on or after 20 November 2010, either by an individual or a company regardless of where it is incorporated, and resold within 24 months would be subject to a sliding scale of SSD levy. Hence, the selected time range excludes the housing transaction records after October 2010 so that the influence, if any, of this anti-speculation special stamp duty on the private residential property market could be excluded from the study to enhance the accuracy of the analytical model.

In our analysis, the unit price of the transacted property flat is selected as the dependent variable in the regression model and the independent variables can be mainly categorized into three groups. The structural group of the independent variables relates to the physical characteristics of the transacted units including building age, floor level as well as gross floor area of the flat. The second group is locational independent variables, which include Kowloon West (denoted as KLW), Kowloon East (KLE), New Territories West (NTW) and New Territories East (NTE), which are categorical dummy variables.

More importantly, a standard dummy variable, which indicates the neighbourhood attribute and represents the existence of an adjacent public housing estate, is inserted to examine the statistical significance of the potential dampening effect of welfare housing. An additional time factor on a monthly basis is taken into consideration, as there might be potential growth in the capital value within the time period under investigation. This independent variable is an index variable running from 1 to 120, representing the transaction dates under the study time frame from 1 November 2000 to 31 October 2010.

Subject private housing developments

In our analysis, a total of eight popular private residential developments, including four in the Kowloon Peninsula and four in the New Territories, are chosen as subject targets for the study. Half of them have adjacent public housing estates in the immediate neighbourhood while the remaining half does not for a controlled comparison. The immediate neighbourhood is defined as a catchment area within a radius of 40 metres from the subject private housing development project.

Traditionally, because of the limited land supply and locational prestigious advantages, the housing values on Hong Kong Island are relatively higher even when comparing to properties with similar physical, structural and neighbouring characteristics on Kowloon Peninsula and in the New Territories. Therefore, residential development projects on Hong Kong Island will not be considered under this study so as to eliminate this inborn price-biased factor in vale differences and to improve the explaining power of the analysis model.

As a number of literatures have pointed out that distance to the nearest subway stations may affect the neighbouring housing price substantially, only those private residential developments located within a similar walking distance to the nearest underground railway (or commonly known as Mass Transit Railway, MTR in Hong Kong) station will be chosen as subject properties. At a normal pace, a person walks approximately 400 metres in five minutes. Therefore, the subject housing projects which fall within the captured zone in a 300-metre radius from any exit of a MTR station will be selected as testing target for this study.

Because the time frame under study is confined to the period between 2000 and 2010, those MTR lines which came into operation after 2000 would be excluded for the investigation. For this reason, only four MTR lines including Kwun Tong Line, Tsuen Wan Line, Tung Chung Line as well as East Rail Line fall within the scope of investigation. In other words, the selected subject private housing projects are all located within a five-minute walking distance next to any one of the stations of these four chosen MTR lines. These private domestic projects are chosen in terms of similarity in size, amenities, neighbouring environment as well as proximity to MTR stations so as to exclude other external factors which affect the property values.

These private housing estates are: Luk Yeung Sun Chuen in Tsuen Wan, Sceneway Garden in Lam Tin, Amoy Gardens in Kowloon Bay, Jubilee Garden in Shatin, Fanling Centre in Fanling, Parc Oasis in Kowloon Tong, Villa Esplanada in Tsing Yi and Island Harbourview in Tai Kok Tsui. On the one hand, these private residential developments are selected owing to the availability of transaction data for them within the time range of investigation. On the other hand, these types of comprehensive private domestic development projects share similar characteristics, such as orientation, accessibility, amenity facilities, design layout and entertainment facilities. Given similar housing characteristics of these residential projects, this can minimize the influences of other external factors affecting their price levels. For this reason, it is quite ideal to make use of them as a controlled comparison for analysis.

The general information of each individual housing estate is briefly summarized in Tables 2.1 and 2.2.

Housing transaction data from these eight popular private housing developments are retrieved from the Economics Property Research Centre (EPRC) database, a commercial database which is commonly used by most academics in Hong Kong because of the comprehensive information it records in each property transaction in the city. There are generally two types of property information provided by the EPRC: the transaction information (such as address, transaction dates as well as transaction prices) and the physical characteristics of the units transacted (such as gross floor area, usable floor area, number of floors, age of the building as well as the date of occupation permit granted). Transaction records from each housing estate for this analysis are listed in Table 2.3.

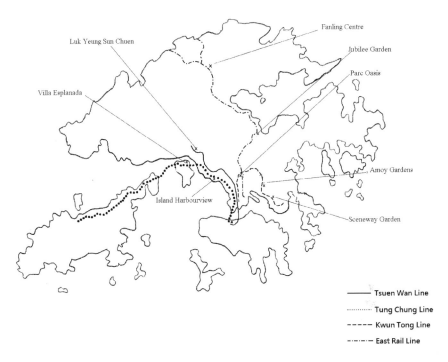

Map 2.1 Location map of the four MTR lines and the six residential communities.

As we can see, except for Amoy Gardens, the number of transaction records for each housing development is also comparable.

A total of 17,297 transaction items from each private housing project for the past 10 years are then merged.

Table 2.1 Details of the four private housing communities on the Kowloon side

Private housing	Amoy Gardens	Sceneway Garden	Parc Oasis	Island Harbourview
District	Kowloon East	Kowloon East	Kowloon East	Kowloon West
Adjacent MTR station	Kowloon Bay, Kwun Tong Line	Lam Tin, Kwun Tong Line	Kowloon Tong, Kwun Tong Line	Olympic, Tung Chung Line
Occupation permit date	06–1987	04–1992	03–1995	05–2000
Number of residential blocks	19	17	32	9
Number of units	4896	4112	1822	2464
Presence of a neighbouring public rental housing community	yes	yes	no	no

Table 2.2 Details of the four private housing communities in the New Territories

Private housing	Luk Yeung Sun Chuen	Jubilee Garden	Fanling Centre	Villa Esplanada
District	New Territories West	New Territories East	New Territories East	New Territories West
Adjacent MTR station	Tsuen Wan, Tsuen Wan Line	Fo Tan, East Rail Line	Fanling, East Rail Line	Tsing Yi, Tung Chung Line
Occupation permit date	05–1984	05–1986	12–1991	11–2000
Property blocks	17	9	11	11
Number of units	4072	2260	2200	2824
Presence of a neighbouring public housing estate	no	no	yes	yes

Dependent variable

The dependent variable PRICE is the transaction price over the gross floor area of the property unit transacted. In order to have a standard unit for comparison purpose, unit price has been adopted. This is calculated by dividing the transaction price by the total gross floor area of housing flat transacted.

Independent variables

A total of seven explanatory variables, including dummy variables, are chosen in the model. In particular, the distance to the nearest MTR station from the subject private housing unit is not taken into consideration. This is because, in the analytical model, the selected residential development projects are already located within the five-minute walking distance from the nearest MTR station.

In order to understand whether and how proximity to subsidized housing community impacts the private residential market, we also need to carry out a micro study in the next stage. In this stage, we will concentrate on the four

Table 2.3 Distribution of data among the eight housing communities in the analysis

Private housing community	Number of property transactions included
Luk Yeung Sun Chuen	2140
Sceneway Garden	2376
Amoy Gardens	4398
Jubilee Garden	1646
Fanling Centre	1619
Parc Oasis	1359
Villa Esplanada	1821
Island Harbourview	1938

communities with an immediate subsidized housing neighbour. We are more interested to find out if the impact of being close to the subsidized housing community is similar to being close to an undesirable facility, such as a refuse collection centre, as explained above. In other words, we hope to find out whether within the same development with a subsidized housing neighbour, those flats which are nearer or having a direct view on the subsidized housing projects will suffer any negative impact in terms of price suppression.

A total of 10,000 housing transactions from these four subject private housing developments are input into the second level analysis. These four private residential property projects all have an adjacent public housing estate neighbour. These four private housing projects are: Sceneway Garden, Villa Esplanada, Amoy Gardens and Fanling Centre.

Outcomes

In the first stage of the study, a total of 17,294 housing transaction records from the eight private residential property development projects in both the New Territories and Kowloon Peninsula are input into the hedonic price model. The regression formula and empirical results of the model are shown as follows:

$$PRICE = C + \alpha*GFA + \beta*FLOOR + \pi*FLOOR^2 + \gamma*AGE + \delta*SEA + \varepsilon*TIME^2 + \eta*PRH + \theta*KLE + \zeta*KLW + \lambda*NTE + \mu*NTW + e$$

Based on Table 2.4, the regression formula of hedonic price model can also be rewritten as follows:

$$PRICE = 2801.0 + 1.9*GFA + 15.2*FLOOR - 0.0003*FLOOR^2 - 18.7*AGE + 160.6*SEA + 0.2*TIME^2 - 2524.2*PRH + 932.9*KLE - 503.7*KLW - 1868.9*NTE - 1357.8*NTW + e$$

Explaining the empirical results

Age of building (AGE)

The AGE is calculated as the difference between the building completion date and transaction date, which could infer a more precise property age of a particular transacted housing unit. As one of the vital structural housing traits, property age can reflect the physical or structural conditions of the building. Other things being equal, the older the property, the poorer the structural condition. Logically, a negative relationship is obtained between AGE and PRICE, as expected, and the resulting coefficient of AGE −18.7.

The negative coefficient of AGE proves that the unit price of private housing is inversely related to property age. The coefficient is of a negative value of −18.7, so we can say that the magnitude of effect of housing age is quite significant.

Table 2.4 Regression outcome of the General Model

Dependent Variable: PRICE
Method: Least Squares
Included observations: 17294

Variable	Coefficient	Std.Error	t-Statistic	Prob.
AGE	−18.70351	1.155992	−16.17961	0.0000*
FLOOR	15.18999	0.612977	24.78069	0.0000*
FLOOR^2	−0.000369	1.49E–05	−24.77606	0.0000*
GFA	1.871756	0.05771	32.43403	0.0000*
PRH	−2524.203	32.418	−77.86422	0.0000*
SEA	160.5504	28.04898	5.723929	0.0000*
TIME^2	0.188156	0.001533	122.706	0.0000*
KLE	932.9063	25.85322	36.08472	0.0000*
NTE	−1868.876	55.06441	−33.93982	0.0000*
KLW	−503.6598	52.47105	−9.598814	0.0000*
NTW	−1357.793	45.20643	−30.0354	0.0000*
C	2801.031	60.19	46.53648	0.0000*
R-squared	0.713526	Mean dependent var		3772.734
Adjusted R-squared	0.713343	S.D. dependent var		1535.451
S.E. of regression	822.0855	Akaike info criterion		16.26226
Sum squared resid	1.17E+10	Schwarz criterion		16.26764
Log likelihood	−140607.8	F-statistic		3913.136
Durbin-Watson stat	1.354829	Prob(F-statistic)		0.000000

Notes:
* represents significant level at 1%

The independent variable is also significant at the 0.01 per cent level, which clearly shows that property age plays a very significant role in housing price.

Gross floor area (GFA)

GFA is one of the essential explanatory variables in the hedonic price model, which reflects the physical size of a housing flat in square metres. The positive coefficient of 1.9 means that housing size is directly correlated with housing value. This implies that the larger the housing flat, the higher the property price.

Time factor (TIME)

The TIME factor has been proved to be a relevant factor, although the magnitude of influence is not significant. This could be the result of the unusual fluctuating market situation during some periods, such as the temporary setback in 2008, when the sub-prime mortgage problem in the US exploded. This also illustrates that the property market in Hong Kong has become relatively mature as people do not uphold the belief that housing price will grow with time constantly forever.

Floor height (FLOOR)

FLOOR refers to the floor level where a particular housing unit in the database is located. In the statistical model, the coefficient of FLOOR is 15.2. This shows a rather important role of floor height in the pricing structure of apartment housing price in Hong Kong. In a compact and densely developed city, such as Hong Kong, it is not unreasonable to expect that people usually prefer a higher floor level to a lower one so as to enjoy a wider and better view, as well as a higher degree of privacy.

Seaview

As expected, the seaview commands a very important role in the price structure of our dataset. The large coefficient of 161 shows that people are willing to pay a premium for a flat with good seaview, compared to other structural housing characteristics.

Public rental housing

Amongst all explanatory variables in the regression formula, public rental housing (PRH) remains the most critical one. This is a dummy variable inserted to indicate the presence or absence of an adjacent public rental housing estate within the immediate neighbourhood of the subject private housing development. The sign of the coefficient is negative from the analysis, which shows that public rental housing projects exert an adverse impact on the private housing market in terms of property price.

The coefficient of PRH variable is −2,524, which is actually the largest in absolute value compared to all other factors in the formula. It illustrates that the negative impact induced by public rental housing is indeed quite substantial in our tests.

Social stigma of public housing in Hong Kong

In this analysis, we observe a negative relationship between public rental housing estates and the neighbouring private housing market in these eight housing communities in Hong Kong. In the next phase, we therefore further investigate the underlying reasons for how public housing exerts an adverse impact on the housing price of the adjacent private residential property community. In an attempt to confirm that the negative impact from public housing is more psychological than physical and observable, another multiple regression model similar to the one in the previous stage will be undertaken by including an additional dummy variable of VIEW. As explained before, the four private housing communities with an immediate public housing neighbour will be examined. In this stage, individual apartment units in these four private housing estates which have a direct view on the neighbouring public rental housing estate will become the target for examination.

In this second stage of the test, only those four private residential developments with adjacent public housing projects are chosen as the subject properties. The four subject private housing developments with public rental housing estate neighbours include Villa Esplanada in Tsing Yi, Sceneway Garden in Lam Tin, Amoy Gardens in Kowloon Bay and Fanling Centre in Fanling. As we could observe, two are on Kowloon Peninsula and two are in the New Territories. This should provide a more balanced view between the urban housing communities and the sub-urban housing communities.

A total of 10,214 housing transaction items are included in this stage of analysis. Table 2.5 summarizes the empirical results.

Based on the above, we observe that the general results of each independent regressor remain more or less the same as the previous regression model. Despite some changes in the coefficient value, the coefficient sign and p-value of individual explanatory variable also remain unchanged. In particular, the newly introduced dummy variable of NT, which represents the housing units in the New Territories or the sub-urban area of Hong Kong, results in a negative coefficient of −1271 as expected. This reflects that housing prices in the sub-urban area of New Territories are generally lower than that in urban Kowloon.

Other statistical indicators, such as the adjusted R-square and F-statistic, show that this second level regression model is highly significant and most independent regressors help explain the movement of property prices in the dataset.

What we are interested in this level of examination is the explanatory variable 'VIEW', which represents a direct view on the neighbouring public rental housing

Table 2.5 Regression outcome of stigma effect analysis

Dependent Variable: PRICE
Method: Least Squares
Included observations: 10214

Variable	Coefficient	Std.Error	t-Statistic	Prob.
GFA	2.086209	0.037238	56.02313	0.0000*
FLOOR	24.17583	1.918558	12.60104	0.0000*
FLOOR^2	−0.272681	0.049775	−5.478222	0.0000*
AGE	−6.236025	0.810843	−7.690788	0.0000*
SEA	311.4811	18.20037	17.114	0.0000*
TIME^2	0.162156	0.001234	131.3123	0.0000*
VIEW	−0.787361	18.01378	1.487048	0.137***
NT	−1270.507	25.95929	−48.94228	0.0000*
C	998.2418	35.67373	27.98255	0.0000*
R-squared	0.754846	Mean dependent var		3344.022
Adjusted R-squared	0.754649	S.D. dependent var		1038.585
S.E. of regression	514.4414	Akaike info criterion		15.32494
Sum squared resid	2.64E+09	Schwarz criterion		15.33143
Log likelihood	−76608.04	F-statistic		3844.978
Durbin-Watson stat	1.251998	Prob(F-statistic)		0.000000

Notes:
* represents significant level at 1%
*** represents significant level at 10%

neighbours from the flats of a particular private housing community. The objective of this examination is to assess if the presence of the public rental housing estate near to a private housing community creates a visual damage. The coefficient of 'VIEW' equals to −0.0787 and the F-Statistic does not pass the threshold of the value '2', which shows the impact is very minimal and insignificant statistically. In other words, the result shows that there is no statistical proof to demonstrate that flats in the private housing community with a direct view on the adjacent public rental housing estates will be selling at a lower value, other things being equal, than flats in the same community without such a direct visual connection. It therefore reinforces Li's study in 2005 that, while in general, people regard neighbouring welfare housing as a negative factor to the price performance of the private housing community, such negative effect, cannot be qualified or rationalized effectively the way one would expect other tangible damage such as proximity to air pollution could be. People who live in a private housing community with a direct welfare housing neighbour do not really feel that being near to this welfare housing community is a threat to their daily life so that they would not pay a premium for flats without a direct view on this welfare housing estate. So, what does this tell us? The moral of this story is that people do feel uncomfortable when they could observe the presence of a lower socio-economic class of residents in their neighbourhood, and sometimes for no substantiated reasons. To break this wall, we need to take away this differentiation when considering the future of public housing programme.

The implications above show that, as long as there is a physical presence of a 'welfare housing community' that the society can physically identify, this problem will persist. To strike the balance, we therefore need a model that will allow the authority to continue housing the poor while the society will not easily notice the presence of this welfare housing group. We take a leap of faith in humanity here and boldly propose the following concept of mixed community.

Mixed community is not a new and noble idea that we have conjured up. The Hong Kong government tried this in the 1990s and failed for various reasons. We would like to resurrect this idea because we feel that, while the government has an obligation to take care of housing problems for those who cannot afford basic shelter, direct involvement in housing production in any market mechanism should proceed with extreme care. More importantly, poverty should not be concentrated physically within the government-built welfare housing projects. As mentioned above, the study by Carter *et al.* (1997) found that public housing programmes initiated by the government in the housing market in the form of public-led supply may actually and unintentionally exert negative impacts on these households.

Consequently, to initiate an effective subsidized housing programme that will serve as a safety net with minimal negative effects noticed by Carter *et al.* (1997) discussed above and that will not be viewed as a direct competition to the private developers especially in a depressed market, the authority needs to consider the following criteria:

1 The subsidized housing programme needs to be seen strictly as a welfare policy, not just as a mechanism to boost homeownership.

2   The subsidized housing programme should have a minimum cost function on government. It should not therefore impose strain on land resources; general construction costs; or future management costs of the completed project.
3   The subsidized housing programme should be as invisible as possible. This means the physical form of the completed subsidized housing projects should not be easily identifiable so as to minimize the social label effect of the traditional perception of 'subsidized' housing as well as the physical presence of government intervention in the market.

An option for such a development model, namely the mixed housing community, is proposed here to address the current housing market problem while satisfying the above criteria as much as socially and politically feasible. It should be emphasized that the concept of mixed housing community is not entirely a new concept in Hong Kong. In February 1998, the Secretary for Housing of the Hong Kong Government published a White Paper on LTHS titled *Homes for Hong Kong People into the 21st Century*, which mentioned this idea. Among all other issues concerning the future development of public housing in Hong Kong, it was considered that the Housing Authority of Hong Kong should look imaginatively at ways in which it can make better use of the private sector's expertise and resources in helping it to deliver its public housing programme. One of the possible options is to invite private developers to build subsidized housing flats, together with ordinary private housing flats on the same site as a mixed development. In this way, a mixed (private and public) housing community will emerge that caters for demand from both the private and public (subsidized for sale, not welfare rental) sectors.

Public housing is usually examined in terms of how the different modes of provision affect the households enjoying this welfare package, as well as how these different modes of welfare housing provision impact on public finances. Ever since the advent of the HOPE programme (Homeownership and Opportunity for People Everywhere) in the US, public housing policy has wider implications than just the physical production of welfare housing package. Provision of welfare/subsidized housing does not have to be confined to specific sites delineated for the subsidized households. Public housing policy can therefore be regarded as a tool to enhance opportunity for specific social groups, or even for the whole community. Subsidized housing and households start to intertwine with the private sector housing community in 'mixed-income neighbourhoods'. The burgeoning study of mixed-income neighbourhoods helps create a wealth of literature that concentrates on this multi-disciplinary study with a focus on using subsidized housing policy as a vehicle to enhance optimal social mix in community development. Casey *et al.* (2007) for example conclude that the concept of 'mixed-tenure housing developed within a carefully planned layout and provision of high-quality neighbourhood facilities' (Casey *et al.*, 2007: 312) is instrumental to more social interaction among different groups of residents within the community, which will lead to higher levels of satisfaction among residents.

Joseph (2010) provides a very interesting prospective on developing mixed-income housing community in the process of urban regeneration from the perspective of private developers in Chicago. A major finding in Joseph's paper is that a mixed-income/mixed-tenure housing community may not easily improve the lives of the lower-class families when they are mixing with middle-class households in the same community, although this development model ends the isolation of lower-income families in specific physical locations labelled with 'subsidized housing'. More interesting, this study finds that developers are not entirely resisting this concept as long as there is adequate support from the government in the whole development inception. A lesson Hong Kong can learn!

Arthurson (2012) shares the view that successful mixed-income/mixed-tenure housing neighbourhoods depend to a certain extent on the design of the housing units, which in turn depends on how indistinguishable the market-rate residential units and the subsidized units are. This issue is also noted in a study by Joseph (2010). Hence, this stigma effect felt by most lower-income families cannot be eliminated if the mixing of welfare and private housing reminds the community of a strong awareness of the existence of the subsidized households. This will undermine the incentive for private developers to participate, as well as the willingness of the lower-income families to be placed in such mixed-income neighbourhoods.

Talen (2008) also agrees that a good design model for the socially mixed neighbourhood could help eradicate the misconception of segregating the rich from the poor households in the society. Hence, it is feasible to promote a more diversified community culture when welfare/subsidized housing can be subsumed in a mixed-income/mixed-tenure housing community, even in a traditionally market-driven economy such as Hong Kong. But special care needs to be taken in the design stage of the neighbourhood as it has been found that market-rate owners and renters do feel negatively towards issues of safety and security in mixed-income neighbourhood, though subsidized families feel improvement in their emotional well-being (Joseph and Chaskin, 2010).

A mixed housing community is essentially a joint venture between the government and a private developer, with the private developer taking a major role in the development process. Under this approach, residential sites NOT in the traditionally high-class residential regions of Hong Kong will be offered for sale by the current open market mechanism, preferable by tender. The successful tenderer is tasked with designing and building flats under a normal private housing development situation. However, as part of the lease conditions, a certain proportion, say not more than 10 per cent of the completed housing flats, will be given to the government as subsidized housing flats for sale to specific income groups classified under the current HOS policy. The government (through its agent) will set the price for the subsidized housing flats and is completely in charge of disposing of these flats. The remaining flats will be retained by the developer as private flats for their own disposal. As an incentive, the 10 per cent of flats may not be counted in the maximum gross floor area in the development, but this is relatively politically sensitive.

The subsidized flats to be returned to the government should be selected at random within the size range set by the HOS policy, instead of a block section to be returned to the government. With the random distribution of subsidized flats in the whole project, the possible social stigmatization associated with public housing projects could be avoided because no geographical boundaries could be drawn between different income groups. It may thus enhance social harmony within the community, as it is not conceivable that all the flats with the worst views and orientation will be designated as subsidized flats. Given the location choice of these sites, it is also not conceivable that there will be a huge discrepancy in social status between the subsidized owners and the market-owners. On the other hand, given the fact that larger flats including duplex units in the community would not be designated as subsidized flats, as the size would exceed the HOS normal design, developers would not fear that their incomes would be substantially decreased if they participated in the scheme.

Advantages

Studies in America have shown that housing production by the public sector can be more expensive than other forms of housing subsidies, such as housing coupons, because the public sector may be more inflexible in dealing with costs. Moreover, the housing voucher scheme adopted in America is based on the policy philosophy of 'Moving to Opportunity',[2] which hopes to allow flexible housing choice for the lower-income groups to move to a neighbourhood where opportunity for them exists. This is one advantage that the traditional supply-led public housing programme cannot afford.

An important principle behind the mixed housing community approach is that all flats will be constructed to the same quality standards and (possibly) within a shorter construction period, regardless of their targeted markets. It would also provide a greater range of product, because of the involvement of different developers building flats to their own design, and therefore more choices for buyers of the subsidized flats. The private sector orientation and different flat types should be very attractive to prospective buyers, particularly from the existing public housing tenants. In terms of management, the completed project can also enjoy higher level of services, especially in the provision of retail and leisure services.

The current land sale programme needs not be substantially amended so as to reserve land for subsidized housing programmes, such as HOS. Land resources including land income can be maintained to a large extent. This also simplifies the market without having to segregate it into too many different sub-sectors.

To the private property flat owners, the scheme will not have a negative impact on property values as it is very difficult to identify which flats belong to the subsidy scheme. Consequently, private flats within the same community will be valued according to the same normal market principle, which even allows the subsidized flats to have a larger database for assessment of premium when the owners subsequently decide to re-sell the flats in the market.

At the same time, the execution of the scheme can be entirely handled by the Housing Authority without any need to expand the current bureaucratic structure. It minimizes financial as well as political costs in execution.

Chapter summary

The above analysis shows that, even in a compact city such as Hong Kong where about half of the population resides in different forms of welfare housing units, the overall housing market still feels uncomfortable to find a welfare housing estate as their neighbour. This uneasiness originates not from measurable physical damage in the way we fear to live near to a nuclear power plant or rubbish landfill. This analysis helps us understand this further – that psychological impact in the property market can be more relevant than the physical impact. This echoes with the observation made at the beginning that some political parties are trapped in this dilemma that, on the one hand, they advocate more welfare housing for the lower-income groups but, on the other, they do not support the location of such welfare housing communities to be near to private housing communities for the benefits of the homeowning middle class.

The Long Term Housing Strategy Committee set up by the Hong Kong Government in 2013 did scratch the surface of the idea of developing mixed-income communities in Hong Kong when it was starting the consultation period in mid 2013. The idea was soon shot down when opposition came from the developers. We would not like to be tangled up in the political debate of the problems of mixing the two sectors of the housing market together, but we feel strongly that there has not been sufficient understanding of this matter in Hong Kong before even a feasibility study of the optimal development model for a mixed-income community could be initiated. However, we realize that housing policy is sometimes too political for idealists!

Notes

1 Exception however can be found in Singapore where public housings are comparable to private housings in terms of living environment and quality.
2 For details, please check: <;http://portal.hud.gov/hudportal/HUD?src=/programdescription/mto>.

3 Children's perception of the built environment

L.H. Li and Hui Sun

Studies around the world have shown that there is a significant correlation between young children's development and the neighbourhood environment in which they are brought up. While the neighbourhood environment is a master set of a vast number of inter-dependent and inter-mingled variables, one particular factor, the physical land use environment, sometimes tends to be overlooked. In fact, all other environmental variables work inside the framework of the land use settings as all human activities take place on and above land and certainly within some form of physical built structure. So, what is built environment, then? The Macmillan Dictionary (online) defines it as 'all the structures people have built when considered as separate from the natural environment'.[1] On the other hand, Wikipedia defines this term as 'a material, spatial and cultural product of human labor that combines physical elements and energy in forms for living, working and playing',[2] and makes reference to a more concise definition by Roof and Oleru (2008) as 'the human-made space in which people live, work, and recreate on a day-to-day basis'. Whatever way we define it, it is beyond argument that the built environment is shaped by man-made structures. These built structures are invariably the consequences of some previous real estate decisions. In this chapter, we will examine how children's perception of their built environment affects one strait of their development, namely academic performance at school.

Introduction

Correlations between environmental attributes and academic performance of children have long attracted interests from environmental psychology, educational psychology and urban design (Evans, 2006). Environmental traits, however, are only part of the larger set of factors that would impact on young people as far as their academic performance is concerned. Academic performance has been known to be influenced by personal characteristics, including intelligence, personality, family and social background, motivation, self-discipline, ability to concentrate and self-esteem (Samdal *et al.*, 1999). Feinstein and Symons (1999) find that parental input, especially parents' interest in children's study, positively impacts on children's academic performance significantly more than schooling input. Because of this matrix of different categories of factors, it will be more meaningful if the focus can be narrowed to certain specific traits for more in-depth discussion. In this chapter, the focus is set on the built environment factors, as it is more complicated to measure the extent of personal, familial and social and educational factors that all have a role in affecting children's academic performance. In addition, direct correlation tests between these environmental factors and actual academic results require a very substantial sample base, as well as a meaningful time series. In this chapter, as an illustration of how real estate decisions shape the built environment, which in turn affects children, we will examine children's 'perception' of the impact of these environmental factors on their academic performance instead.

Nevertheless, the built environment is still a very large topic to review. In this chapter, therefore, we limit the examination to children's primary environment. According to Stokols (1976), the primary environment is defined as where one spends a great deal of time and where one establishes important personal relationships, such as home, work place, school and childcare centres. Weinstein (1979) is one of the research pioneers in this area of research. According to his research, he examines the impact of six different classroom environmental variables, namely seating position, classroom design, density, privacy, noise and the presence or absence of windows, on students' behaviour, attitudes and achievement and finds these factors to be important and influential.

The environmental psychology of childhood and adolescence is still a new and developing field. Brooks-Gunn *et al.* (1997) suggest that careful attention should be paid when examining the influence of the neighbourhood on children's development. Three issues need to be considered when conducting research. First, what constitutes the neighbourhood-level condition should be considered. Second, a sufficient number of samples should be included in the research. Third, multilevel models, longitudinal approaches and combining quantitative and qualitative approaches are recommended.

According to Brooks-Gunn *et al.* (1997), although research on neighbourhood has prospered, there are still a lot of theoretical, conceptual and methodological issues that have not been resolved. Gifford and Lacombe (2006) examine the correlation between the socio-emotional health of children in the age group of 9–12 years old and the physical quality of their own residence and neighbourhood in Canada. They show that there are important connections between housing quality and socio-emotional health of children measured in terms of behavioural problems. The socio-emotional health of children is shown to depend on the physical condition of their residence's interior, exterior and immediate neighbourhood. The relation is more significant after controlling for household income, parental education and mental health status, the child's gender and time lived in the residence. This result is shared by other researchers such as Evans *et al.* (2003). Li (2009) also notes the existence of a correlation between certain housing conditions and children's academic performance in the public examination in Hong Kong. Hence, housing and children are two inter-related issues that warrant more multi-disciplinary studies.

In the study of the impact of 'home environment', Evans (2006) shows that individuals who had their own room during childhood tend to have a much smaller probability than others of dropping out of school before earning a diploma. Children suffer fewer ill effects in a noisy or crowded home if they have a room of their own. Li (2009) notes that, in Hong Kong, families that can afford to provide personal space to their children are able to reinforce the concentration of such children in their own study time, leading to relatively good results in the public examinations. On the other hand, frequent home movement also has an impact on children's scholastic achievement (Brooks-Gunn *et al.*, 1997).

Sociologists and social psychologists have long been interested in the problems caused by overcrowded housing (Maxwell, 2003). Parents are less responsive to young children in more-crowded homes, irrespective of social class. Reduced parental monitoring of children also occurs in higher density homes. Evans (2006) finds that there is a correlation between young children's aggression and home density. Again, housing policy in the macro set of real estate research should not just concentrate on the supply side mechanism in terms of the most efficient way to produce the maximum number of affordable flats. Housing policy should therefore also consider the impact of public housing and community design.

In terms of 'neighbourhood environment', Evans (2006) points out that several adverse child outcomes are related to residence in economically impoverished neighbourhoods. Mueller and Tighe (2007) find that girls residing in housing near to natural outdoor spaces show better attention and emotional self-regulating ability. Outdoor activities in the natural environment also benefit children. Nature near the housing community may also enhance children's attention and may act as a buffer against some of the ill effects of chronic stress exposure among children. This final aspect echoes with the current debate in Hong Kong, as well as in other densely developed cities, on converting country-park sites into housing development sites to solve the high housing demand in the city. This delicate balance between conservation and solving housing demand is not easy to strike when taking the impact of the natural environment on children into consideration.

Weinstein (1979) reports that children who are exposed to noise at home suffer greater reading problems and cognitive delay. The effects of noise on children's cognition are found to be related to more central information processes. Gump (1987), in his study of Chicago's Gautreaux program and other mobility programs, concludes that the location of residence and schools in dangerous neighbourhoods can have a negative impact on children's attitudes toward school. The school environment is perceived as the medium through which teachers help children to engage attention and concentrate (Samdal *et al.*, 1999). Research on the school environment's influence on students' academic performance identifies specific environmental variables on children's school attainment, including acoustics and noise, lighting, temperature, seating position, classroom furnishing layouts and design, windows, class size and density, school size and open versus traditional classrooms (Weinstein, 1979).

In fact, there is considerable evidence that the physical environment can affect behaviour and attitude of both teachers and students (Gump, 1987). The physical environment plays an indirect role in student achievement (Moore and Lackney, 1993). Research shows that a comfortable, attractive physical setting can create

Photo 3.1 Kindergarten situated near to a market, a very common situation in Hong Kong.

enthusiasm for learning and positive social relationships (Samdal *et al.*, 1999). The positive attitudes and behaviour of children can positively influence their academic performance. The positive attitudes and behaviours of the teachers will benefit the student–teacher relationship resulting in better student achievement.

In addition, there is substantial literature considering the effect of noise on children's learning (Wilensky, 2002). A number of studies have discovered that noise is related to reading problems (O'Neill and Oates, 2001) and more general cognitive deficits among children. Furthermore, teachers in noisy schools report greater fatigue, annoyance, and less patience (Tanner, 2000). All of these point to the fact that the decision on where to locate schools goes beyond just a land use planning consideration. In this way, educational policy and land use policy cross paths where the public authority could utilize a better-designed built environment to foster better learning outcomes among children.

Real estate research and child development

In this chapter, we will apply the Analytical Hierarchy Process (AHP) developed by Saaty (1996) to illustrate the perception of young children in Hong Kong about environmental attributes to their academic performance. We cannot emphasize enough that we do not intend to analyse child development as a whole. Our intention is to apply the AHP model to provide another angle to understand how children perceive the importance of the built environment in relation to their learning outcomes. AHP is a 'decision hierarchy, containing a goal or mission statement, objectives or criteria, and alternatives of choice' and 'is evaluated by deriving ratio-scale priorities from pair-wise judgments' (Saaty and Niemira, 2006: 1). Such perception tends to be more intangible, although quantifiable.

In carrying out the AHP analysis, there is a need to develop the hierarchy of attributes. In this study, we elaborate two levels of this hierarchy:

Level 1: Categories

As noted above, school, home and neighbourhood environments form the three basic components in children's primary environment. Therefore, a simplified hierarchy with these three categories in level 1 is suggested.

Level 2: Factors

Eighteen factors, under the three categories, are considered to exert impact on students' academic performance in Hong Kong. Such academic performance is using the proxy of the public examination known as the Hong Kong Certificate of Education Examination, or HKCEE. The time-honoured HKCEE system was abolished in 2010 when the education system in middle school and universities in Hong Kong was overhauled at the same time. According to Saaty (1996), most people only have the capacity to deal with approximately seven (plus or minus two) variables when processing information. Hence, although a large number of built environment factors may influence the school-children's HKCEE perfor-mance, only the relatively important factors will be chosen for the hierarchy. Thus we need some principles in deciding the factors of level 2.

The principles in deciding on the structure of the level 2 in the hierarchy are:

1   Each factor should represent a distinct aspect of the built environment.
2   It is possible to assess the relative importance of these factors when their influence on HKCEE is considered.
3   The factors should represent the built environment of the respective cate-gory. Repetition in assessment should be avoided.

In this study, factors influencing the secondary students' HKCEE score are attained from the criteria established by the American Public Health Association (APHA) in 1945 in setting out measurement of housing, as well as other subsequent related work (Evans *et al.*, 2001 and Gifford and Lacombe, 2006). The factors in the ques-tionnaire are based on the three principles above. Consequently, we have developed the following matrix of factors in level 2 as depicted by Figure 3.1 opposite.

Real estate research and the impact of the built environment

In this study, three groups of university students from The University of Hong Kong (HKU), The Hong Kong Polytechnic University (PolyU) and The Hong

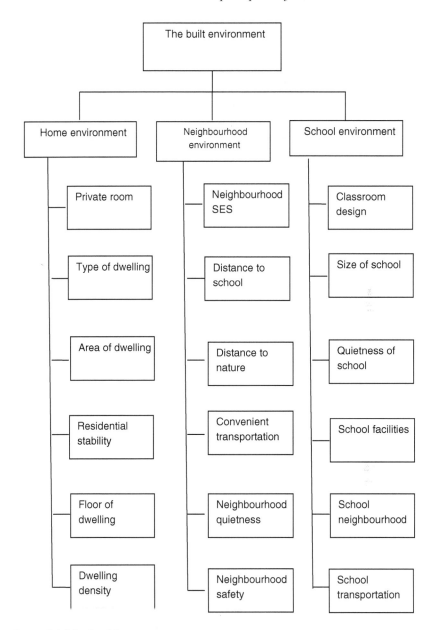

Figure 3.1 Matrix of factors.

Kong Institute of Education (HKIE) were asked to participate in the survey during the period October and November 2008. These groups of respondents were randomly chosen from these three universities. These students were asked to recall their perception of the various environmental traits that (they regarded) helped shape their Hong Kong Certificate Education Examination (HKCEE) performance when they were in high school two years before. Although this public examination does not exist anymore, it does not reduce the reliability of this analysis as HKCEE scores are adopted here as a proxy only. Students from different institutions were mainly selected because of the need to seek a balanced distribution of HKCEE results: 57 copies from HKU, 43 copies from PolyU and 34 copies from HKIE. Hence, a total of 134 valid questionnaires were collected in this analysis.

The respondents were given a questionnaire which contains five parts. The first part asks the respondents to make pair-wise comparisons of the three categories regarding their importance to the respondents' HKCEE score. The respondents were also asked to rate the level of importance from 1 to 5. Parts Two, Three and Four of the questionnaire ask the respondents to make pair-wise comparisons of six factors under the home built environment, neighbourhood built environment and school built environment respectively. Part Five is the respondents' background information and includes their HKCEE score and the other demographic information.

Data

In the literature of environmental psychology, the development of male and female children depends on the environment in different ways. In this study, the distribution between male and female participants is quite even. With close to equal sampling of male and female participants, this study equally reflects the perception of male and female students.

The HKCEE scores are divided into five score groups: 6–10; 11–15; 16–20; 21–25; 26–30. A higher point means a better grade; 30 is the highest grade. We can see from Figure 3.2 that most of the respondents are in the 16–20 group; which is in the middle level of the total grade point. There are more than 30 per cent of participants in the 16–20 group, and there are more than 20 per cent of participants falling

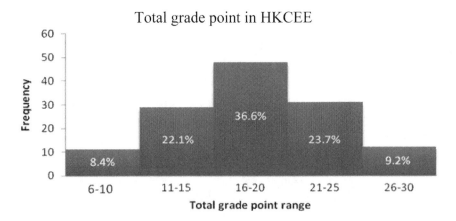

Figure 3.2 HKCEE score range in our dataset.

Table 3.1 Respondents' secondary school distribution

District of secondary school	Number of respondents' school	Number of schools in the district	Participant percentage
Tuen Mun	20	46	43.48
Sha Tin	13	50	26.00
Kwai Chung & Tsing Yi	9	43	20.93
North	7	41	17.07
Kowloon City	17	101	16.83
Wan Chai	7	47	14.89
Hong Kong East	8	54	14.81
Southern	5	38	13.16
Tai Po	3	31	9.68
Kwun Tong	6	72	8.33
Sham Shui Po	5	63	7.94
Yau Tsim & Mong Kok	6	79	7.59
Wong Tai Sin	6	80	7.50
Tsuen Wan	4	54	7.41
Yuen Long	6	82	7.32
Sai Kung	3	45	6.67
Central & Western	3	49	6.12
Total	128	975	13.10

into the 11–15 and 21–25 group. Only less than 10 per cent of participants are in the less than 10 or more than 26 group.

This distribution shows that the sampling of this survey is representative enough of different levels of students, so it equally reflects the perception of students with different academic abilities.

In this survey, respondents graduated from 17 different secondary schools in all the districts in Hong Kong, except the relatively remote Island district. These districts can be divided into four groups. The first group is from Tuen Mun district and they account for about 43.48 per cent of the total sample. In the second group more than 20 per cent of participants are from Kwai Chung & Tsing Yi and Sha Tin districts. The third group are students from Hong Kong South, Hong Kong East, Wan Chai, Kowloon City and the North districts which accounts for approximately 10 per cent of participants are from these districts. Finally, less than 10 per cent of the participants are from the other districts in Hong Kong, except for the Island district.

Davis-Kean (2005) and Brooks-Gunn *et al.* (1997) have shown that parents' education is important in predicting the achievement of children. They point out that one parent's education background influences the academic achievement of the children. Table 3.2 shows that more than half of the respondents' parents acquired middle school education and the second majority of their parents have acquired primary school education. Few parents attended college, postgraduate or above education. Thus, the respondent parents' education backgrounds are very similar. The similar education background of the participants' parents in this study could reduce its influence on this survey.

Table 3.2 Distribution of parents' education level

	No. of fathers' education level	No. of mothers' education level
Master or above	6	1
College	10	9
Middle school	75	76
Primary school	39	45

Built environment factors weights results

This part presents the analyses on the built environment perceptions data obtained from the survey. Computer software is used to process the preference of each of the 134 respondents for the built environment factors through pair-wise comparisons. The consistency ratio (CR) is the degree of inconsistency computed by the computer programme for each set of data. In the AHP framework, inconsistency indicates the variability of human perception. Generally, if the CR is less than 0.1, the result is acceptable. The lower the CR, the better the results. The average inconsistency rate (geometric mean) in this study is 0.012.

A summary of the average factor weights and ranks for all the respondents is presented in Table 3.3. It shows the overall ranking of each factor in descending order of importance. The top five of the 18 built environment factors account for more than 50 per cent of the importance. These five factors are: quietness of school, school facilities, school transportation, school neighbourhood and residential

Table 3.3 Overall ranking and geometric mean of factor weights from all respondents

Factor	*Overall factor weights*	*Overall ranking*
Quietness of school	0.137	1
School facilities	0.136	2
School transportation	0.116	3
School neighbourhood	0.093	4
Residential stability	0.079	5
Size of school	0.068	6
Private room	0.063	7
Classroom design	0.055	8
Dwelling density	0.049	9
Area of dwelling	0.039	10
Neighbourhood safety	0.029	11
Type of dwelling	0.028	12
Neighbourhood quietness	0.027	13
Convenient transportation	0.027	14
Distance to school	0.019	15
Floor of dwelling	0.017	16
Distance to nature	0.008	17
Neighbourhood SES	0.008	18
Total	1	N/A

stability. The top four factors belong to school environment and residential stability (5th) belongs to home environment.

The weights rather than the factor rank are used to represent the children's perception on the built environment because the difference between weights could be diminutive although the rank is different.

School environment

School facilities and quietness of the school are ranked as the top two factors in the hierarchy, meaning that the respondents believe these two factors to be the most important to affect their HKCEE score. Lemasters (1997) in his synthesis studies concludes that there is a positive relationship between school facilities and students' achievements. Hong Kong is a very busy city and a lot of schools are located in the noisy districts with a lot of traffic which could impact negatively on the study environment. However, students need a quiet place to focus on their study. It is not surprising that the survey participants believe that quietness of school is the most important factor which influences their HKCEE score.

Classroom design is the least important factor among the school environment category. This is because almost all classrooms in conventional local schools in Hong Kong are designed in very much the same way. This more or less neutralizes the impact of classroom design on students' performance. It will be interesting of course if schools with very different classroom design such as internationals schools can be included in future studies of similar kind.

Home environment

It is very surprising to find that residential stability is the fifth most important factor among these 18 factors and the most important factor among all other home environment factors. Residential stability is not a very topical research area in Hong Kong, compared to overseas. By residing in the same neighbourhood, children can stay in the same school, live in the same neighbourhood and play with the same group of friends. If the home environment is changing all the time, children will face a lot of problems in adjusting to new neighbourhood and school environment as well as new friendship. In this perspective, residential stability is an important factor to keep the children in a stable study environment.

On the other hand, private room (ranked 7th) at home is found to be a very crucial factor in the home environment. The respondents also express that a private room at home is important to their HKCEE performance. The importance of a private room is not only felt on their study, but also on their need for personal privacy. Children for their own personal development need a private place to study, to think, to build their self-esteem and, in the age of Internet, interact with their peers online. Li (2009) confirms the importance of the private room and states that crowdedness at home has a negative effect on academic performance.

Nevertheless, dwelling density (ranked 9th) and size of dwelling (ranked 10th) are of average importance to the HKCEE performance. A private room is apparently more important than these two factors. It implies that, even if families have a small apartment, it is much more important for parents to allow for children's privacy in order to improve their academic performance.

More interestingly, the type of dwelling (ranked 12th in the analysis) is not as important as expected in affecting children's academic performance. Conventional wisdom tells us that the types of dwelling represent the children's neighbourhood socio-economic status (SES). From our analysis, we can see that neighbourhood SES only plays a minor role in our respondents' HKCEE score. There are a number of reasons behind this, and one of them could be the fact that there are families living in the private sector's sub-divided flats, which are usually in a dilapidated state, and that their socio-economic status may not be substantially higher than those living in the public housing estate. Similarly, there could be relatively affluent families living in the public housing community. Without further data on the actual family incomes and financial status, this variable is not entirely representative in our analysis.

Neighbourhood environment

Neighbourhood safety (ranked 11th) is found to be the most important factor among the neighbourhood environment group of factors. In the survey, a lot of students mentioned that neighbourhood safety is very important to them. In a safe community, they can go out without feeling any threat. They can also study with their friends in community libraries and self-study centres.

Convenient transportation (ranked 13th) and neighbourhood quietness (ranked 14th) have very similar weighting values as neighbourhood safety. These three factors are in fact closely related to each other, as convenient transportation means minimal walking distance from home. Neighbourhood quietness also means less chance of street gangs gathering around their community.

Finally, neighbourhood Social Economic Status (SES) (18th) and distance to nature (17th) are the least important factors in our analysis. Evans (2006) points out that access to nearby nature is beneficial to learning experience. But in this survey distance to nature ranked very low. This might be a common phenomenon in an urban city, such as Hong Kong, where most children do not spend enough time in enjoying nature, not to mention that a lot of country parks are not accessible by children on their own.

In summary, the neighbourhood environment category only ranks less than 15 per cent among these three categories of the built environment attributes which influence the students' HKCEE score. This is not difficult to explain because Hong Kong is such a compact city with very limited open space in most neighbourhoods. It is not easy to expect students to be spending time in the neighbourhood other than commuting from home to other places.

Policy implications of the analysis

School location choice and school land use policy

Educational policy may find interest from this research through improvements to educational (physical) settings such as school, home and neighbourhood in order to promote academic performance of children. School environment is perceived to be the most important environment according to the participants in terms of its ability to improve students' academic performance among home, neighbourhood and school environment. Students, after all, spend most of their study time at school.

School features can enhance students' academic achievement. If students are to perform well, they need places which allow them to concentrate when they study. Among various school environment factors, quietness of school is seen as one of the most important factors, followed by school facilities.

Students are disturbed by street and other outside noises, which decrease their academic performance. Research has found that exposure to noisy urban streets leads to significant increases in blood pressure and reduces the ability of students to concentrate on their studies (Moore and Lackney, 1993). Blood pressure and concentration are important mediators of academic outcomes. The appropriate location of new schools should consider this noise-related problem.

The government and society should provide a quiet location for schools within the availability of suitable sites. Good academic achievement instigates high satisfaction at school which in turn contributes to the students' motivation and incentive to good performance.

Generally, Hong Kong public schools are located in the crowded and noisy areas of the city, with a lack of greenery, play areas, rest places, natural places and other resources for children's healthy growth. This is mainly because convenience is a main factor for school location as most students rely on public transportation to commute to and from schools. This is quite a contrast with some international schools and a few local schools which are lucky enough to locate in a nice and even natural environment. When the government and its urban planners consider the school location choice, it is strongly recommended that the school should be located in a quiet place, equipped with suitable facilities. City planners can use these results during pre-design research in order to investigate the needs of the users: students and teachers. Policy makers, urban design and educational professionals should consider the impact of noise in school site, school facilities and school transportation.

Improve school facilities

The main objectives of schooling are personal development and academic achievement. Students' academic achievement is regarded as a measure of a school's effectiveness.

School is like a microcosm of society, or a cooperative community, containing scaled-down versions of adult activities. Following this metaphor, architects have imaginatively organized the schools as a microcosm of the city with classrooms as houses, corridors and communal spaces as streets, and the assembly hall as a town hall or place of public life.

Lemasters (1997) concludes that school facilities which are well-maintained impact on students' achievement positively. It has been confirmed in this research as well. School facilities are rated as one the most important factors affecting students' academic performance. Weinstein (1979) concludes that the physical environment affects attitudes, and positive attitudes may result in improved achievement.

This analysis shows that the level of 'school facilities' is one of the two important built environment factors which affect children's academic performance. Many architects have done a great deal of practical work in school facilities management in Hong Kong. A library equipped with computer network facilities will hold a crucial role in the school and provide a place for students to pursue self-learning. In addition to libraries, sports facilities and arts studio are also important for the full development of the students.

School architecture can support and motivate students to be academically successful within a complex social environment. For urban designers, physical learning environments should be more 'teacher- and learner-friendly'. Some school psychologists recognize the impact of environment on student behaviour, but this issue is often not considered when designing schools. The basic unit of school facilities is the classroom. In the modern education system, children-centred or subject-centred curricula are important. Teachers need a well-defined, orderly classroom environment that serves as a safe haven for children in order to be more effective educators. However, education needs both learning through social interaction in the classroom, and learning through disciplinary methods. Different kinds of teaching methods and learning modes require different types of classroom design and size. These conflicting educational demands create competing design requirements, such as requirement of distance and separation of activity on the one hand, and the requirement for compactness and flexibility of space on the other. Classroom designers need to better understand the needs of this situation. Dudek (2000) for example suggests a 'hybrid approach' to teaching that reflects a range of views on how children learn. He finds that it is not simply either child-centred or teacher-centred, but should be both at the same time.

Outside the classroom, school grounds deserve more attention as another site for education. Malone and Tranter (2003), for example, have identified the importance of school grounds in children's environment education drawing on the findings of a project which was carried out in five Australian schools.

Housing policy

Residential instability has a strong negative influence on children's academic performance. As we can see from the survey, residential stability is the most influential factor which influences students' academic performance among home and neighbourhood environmental factors.

Providing decent housing for poor families is a good means to improve children's immediate environment, and consequently positively affect their school performance. The best way to improve the living condition of poor children is to help children' access to public library or other recreational facilities, which could further improve their academic performance and other non-academic behaviour at school. With this help, children from low-income families could have a better chance to get into universities and build a better career path. Therefore, public housing policy, whether rental or HOS-type, should aim at helping lower-income families first, who have a much stronger and imminent housing need than other groups.

Chapter summary

Children's academic performance is influenced by many intrinsic and exogenous factors. Intrinsic factors such as students' intelligence directly affect their learning outcome and play substantial roles in their academic performance. Exogenous factors such as students' living and studying environment, on the other hand, may act indirectly on students' academic performance by influencing their behaviour and study attitude. These extrinsic factors have been shown to have considerable, and sometimes crucial, importance to children academic performance (Buckey *et al.*, 2004; Evans, 2006).

Built environment in the context of children's development refers to the primary living and study environment of children, including home environment, neighbourhood environment and school environment. Previous studies have identified built environment factors such as noise level, classroom density, etc. to be relevant to children's academic performance. A systematic classification and evaluation of the importance of these built environment factors, however, remains a problem to be addressed, especially in a compact city such as Hong Kong.

Pragmatically, this study contributes to a general understanding of the influence of the built environment to children's public examination performance, especially during the period of their adolescence. Understanding of certain real estate elements in our society does contribute to the other social aspects.

The leading importance of school environment factors implies that most students are prone to changes in the school environment. The relevant factors belonging to this category may be far beyond the scope investigated here to include other non-physical factors such as peer relationship, teacher attitude, parents' education background and so on.

This study has built a hierarchy of 18 built environment factors and investigated their impact on students' academic performance in Hong Kong. This is one of the few attempts to take into account both Hong Kong's education system and its urban landscape. The results of this survey provide a link between children's development and urban planning. For example, it shows the importance of school quietness and easy access, which could be mutually exclusive factors, and should be considered in choosing a new school site or making an urban development plan around an existing school. In general the relative importance of built environment factors obtained in this study has crucial implications for the urban land policies, especially those related to school location or school neighbour-hood. It also provides an important reference for resource allocation in the making of government policy.

Notes

1 Source: <http://www.macmillandictionary.com/dictionary/british/the-built-environment>.
2 Source: <http://en.wikipedia.org/wiki/Built_environment>.

4 Environment and children – how do children sense their land use environment?

L.H. Li

Eight years ago I happened to meet an educational specialist in Australia, who introduced the concept of the Child Friendly City to me and then I read somewhere that in Africa, there is a saying 'it takes a village to raise a child'. This may not be entirely agreeable in our Chinese culture, but there is a certain degree of truth. 'Child development' is a very specific term referring to the physical and psychological development of children. Child development and real estate research should have no overlapping area in principle, as most people would think child development is more about humanity while real estate research is more about maximizing investment return for the rich! But then, if real estate is interpreted as the use of buildings and land, it fits perfectly well into this multi-disciplinary research agenda. This is because children spend a large amount of their time at home and the immediate housing environment in return has a strong impact on them. In this chapter, we will continue with our discussion on the built environment and children from the previous chapter and extend the focus to look at how they view the overall physical form of our society, which, as I keep emphasizing, is shaped by various real estate decisions.

Introduction

Research in children and the built environment can be traced back to the 1960s and 70s with the pioneer work by Jacobs (1964), followed by the influential work from Lynch (1977). Starting from Wilson's *The Truly Disadvantaged* (1987), sociologists have started to realize that poor environments in the inner urban neighbourhoods contribute a lot to the 'natural disadvantages' facing the poor families living in these neighbourhoods. Hence 'ecological context mattered in very fundamental ways that went beyond individual characteristics or family circumstances' (Massey, 2001: 42). The tenet that environment is an important factor in an individual's personal development is firmly established. In the recent decades, research interests in the aspect of the correlation between neighbourhood environment and young people's development have spun off into a variety of foci on the physical environment of urban space for children (Torrell, 1990), on the social (Hart, 1997) and legal view (Eekelaar, 1986) of youth's participation in urban planning, as well as on the urban safety for young people (Blakeley, 1994).

All these imply an apparent inadequacy in the understanding of the needs of our young children who by no means should be regarded as second-class citizens as far as decisions on and management of the urban space are concerned.

Urban space is essential for young people to experience the path of growing up in the adult's world. The *Skeffington Report* published in 1969 notes that 'the education of secondary school children about aspects of community life offers the best foundation for worthwhile participation in the years to come' (Skeffington, 1969: para. 244). Consider that most of community activities take place within the settings of urban space and within a physical built environment shaped by urban planning, land use and real estate policies; this experience path of young people should be encouraged and taken more seriously. Simpson (1997) notes the legal and social problems in constraining such experience to be enjoyed by our younger generation. He explains that in most societies young children are not regarded as legally equal to an adult and children are mostly treated as 'future citizens' who should not be given a place in the 'current' decision making process for urban space planning. As a result, children are often denied access to voice their needs in urban planning and land use policies, which affect substantially their childhood development. Simpson remarks this consequence quite concisely that 'empowering "users" is disconnected from the benefits for children, who apparently are not "users" in the same sense as other members of the community' (Simpson, 1997: 918).

In practical terms, such a denial of young people's needs in the production of urban space has excluded young people from the broader category of 'public' in the enjoyment of open space for their own activities. Valentine (1996) notes that open space can sometimes be 'closed' space where young people are subject to adults' interpretation of acceptable mode of behaviour and rules of usage in such areas. This drives young people away from the 'adults' open space and the results can be more chaotic' (Valentine, 1996: 214). One should come to realize that young people are in fact one of the most frequent user groups of open/public space in our society given their less-constrained time management, although it is true that most essential urban economic activities involve adults only, especially in the central business district (CBD).

Even though one may argue that urban space to a large extent is more valuable to adults than to young children, one cannot delineate urban open space as 'adult-public' domain only. Lasch (1995) stresses the important of informal meeting places where children can learn from unrelated adults interacting with each other and assuming responsibility in the neighbourhood, something they don't teach young kids in schools.

Measurement of collective neighbourhood effects on children's development has gained tremendous success with the application of econometric and other quantitative analyses (Duncan and Raudenbush, 1999; and Sampson *et al.*, 1997). Brooks-Gunn *et al.* (1997) for example apply regression models in their study to explain the correlations between the socio-economic characteristics of neighbourhoods and developmental outcomes of children with interesting results. While the examination of these socio-economic factors in the neighbourhood is essential and instrumental to the understanding of neighbourhood effects on children, researchers on children development have also agreed that the impact of urban land use patterns/systems on children's well being has often been overlooked. Sampson (2001), explains very succinctly about the potential effect of such 'routine activities'[1] perspective that '… the mix of residential with commercial land use, public transportation nodes… are relevant to organizing how and when children come into contact with other peers, adults, and nonresident activity…' (Sampson, 2001: 11).

Experiencing urban Hong Kong

Urban space is essential for young people to experience the path of growing up in the adult's world. Most urban activities take place on and above land, this experience should be encouraged. For some people, the term 'urban experience' may sound intriguingly confusing. When we set out and attempt to 'experience' something, we normally try to feel something that does not occur to us daily. We therefore will experience new challenges by trying sky-diving or simply a new hairstyle for the graduation party, or experience a new life style when we move to a completely new environment. However, for city dwellers, we do live in an urban environment for the most part of our conscious life and we don't regard daily routine matter to be an 'experience'.

To explore how young people 'experience' our urban environment, I did a simple experiment with a team of young people from different family back-grounds in the age group of 15–18 a few years ago. In this interesting task, they are asked to visit a number of places, including old and high-class residential districts, business district, industrial area and recreational area. In each spot, they are asked to write down their feelings about planning, design, transportation, provision of facilities, and their feeling on the local residents/passers-by. Table 4.1 depicts the extracts from the text records from the young people in Hong Kong on their feelings of Central, the CBD in HK. The texts from their 'CBD experience' are selected for this chapter because they show an interesting diversity of views from different young people in this commercial district in Hong Kong.

One can notice from the Table 4.1 how different young people see the CBD, known as the Central, in Hong Kong. The spectrum ranges from love to loath. What makes these particular young people form such a view on a commercial district is an interesting social research, and to a certain extent it is also related to their own familial and personal background. For instance, it is very likely that children from upper-middle-class families, who may have visited Central quite often with their families, may tend to have a more positive feeling about Central than children from the lower working class, who may not have a lot of opportunities to visit Central in their own time. In any case, it seems as a government, we do need to know more about how our younger generation feels about the overall built environment. To achieve this aim, we expand our analysis to include more children with a more systematic set of questions than this 'urban experience' exercise.

Youngsters' view on the built environment

Between February and March 2002, we conducted a series of large-scale ques-tionnaire surveys covering six secondary schools in various districts and one

Table 4.1 Views of young people from their 'Central experience'

Mui	Ray	Ki	Me
Central always known as the wealthy district and *only people with good knowledge can work here and they do not wear casual dress.* People over Central walk very fast and they produce a special image to me, people all fighting with time and always in a rush. I seldom visit Central as the things sold in Central are not suitable for me.	I seldom go to Central as the *district gives people a sense of suppression* with all these buildings and the pace of life there. Besides, the goods in these fancy shops in Central are out of our league.	Everybody in Central seems to be carrying the word 'busy' on their face and they always move very fast. They cross the road fast and they eat fast. *They feel cold to me though. I guess they cannot afford to notice what is going on around* and even when an old lady trips and falls, they could not care less. The day I visited, there was actually an old lady trying to cross the road without following the light. Nobody seems to feel the need to stop her. *Everybody seems to be talking to themselves and Central is too cold for me.*	Ever since I was a little girl, Central gives me a sense of 'highness'. The buildings are tall, rentals are high and there are a lot of high-class shops. *I like Central as it is like a kaleidoscope, it is so colourful and full of different things.* When you walk into Central, you find it fascinating. I feel proud of HK for being a truly international financial hub. *I wish one day I will work here as I think only those who are talented and successful can work here.*

private tutoring school in Hong Kong. Because the survey was conducted in cooperation with these schools, the return rate was satisfactory. A total of 3,128 questionnaires were returned for analysis covering the youngsters in the 13–18 age group. A number of questions were asked mainly on their views of the ways they interact with the built environment and with their own housing community. The objectives are to examine the extent to which young people like/dislike the physical environments; to examine the optimal land use pattern and policy that will maximize young people's needs and to encourage young people to be more aware of their physical environment.

Forty-four per cent of the respondents are male students and 56 per cent are female. Eighty-two per cent of the respondents were born in Hong Kong while 15 per cent and 3 per cent were born in mainland China/Macau and other places respectively. In terms of their living environment, 19.5 per cent live in public housing estate, 10.5 per cent in Home Ownership Scheme housing units (HOS) (subsidised public-sector housing which is built for sale to middle/lower income group),

38.1 per cent in private housing sector, 0.1 per cent in temporary housing environment, 3.8 per cent in non-domestic buildings such as job-attached staff quarter and 16.3 per cent in non-specified buildings, and the rest refused to disclose.

The qualitative analysis is conducted in two levels. In the first level analysis, responses of these young people are compiled to examine the tendency of their views in aggregate on several issues relating to the built environment, community and land use policy. In the second level analysis, we segregate the youngsters into four categories by the nature of their residential neighbourhoods. Accordingly, the first group contains young people from the public housing (rental housing) neighbourhoods, the second group is the subsidised public-sector housing which is built for sale to middle/lower income group, or the so-called HOS project in Hong Kong, private housing is the third category and non-domestic housing neighbourhood such as job-related staff quarters and indefinable neighbourhoods belong to the 'others' category. The second level analysis is to provide a cross-category examination in order to show whether these young people from different neighbourhoods will share the same feelings towards the above land use/built environment effect issues. Because of the potential problem of the 'others' category in providing a generalized background of neighbourhood, we will concentrate on the first three groups only.

Role of public space in the community

It has been argued in various ways (Jacobs, 1964; Katz, 1994; Coley *et al.*, 1997; and Kelly and Becker, 2000) that public open space serves an important role in good community planning practice not just as provision of 'physical space', but also as a medium for residents' interaction. Young people in our survey share the same view as the majority of them agree that the existence of a large public open space/plaza type of structure will foster interactions among community residents. On the other hand, only a slight majority of them feel such public open space in their housing estate would enhance interaction among family members (see Tables 4.2–4.5). Furthermore, when asked whether public open space in their neighbourhood (75 per cent of them can identify such an open space in their community) has created a friendly community, only 41 per cent agree and 24 per cent of them hold an opposite view, with 35 per cent being neutral on this. This failure to confirm the positive role of public open space is also observed in the response from another question about whether public open space has induced residents to be more caring about their neighbours. In this aspect, only a low 32 per cent agree, with a matching 28 per cent disagree, in addition to a high 40 per cent neutral category. It shows that it takes more than the mere provision of the physical public open space to achieve better community outcomes.

In this respect, it is interesting to note that young people from different social-economic neighbourhoods differ slightly in their views. It seems that apart from the issue of public open space being able to foster more interaction among residents, proportionately more young people from the private residential neighbourhoods tend to enjoy the positive outcomes brought about by the public open space in their neighbourhoods than those from the public/subsidized housing neighbourhoods.

Table 4.2 Public open space will foster interaction among residents in the community

	Yes (%)	Neutral (%)	No (%)
Overall response	50.4	32.2	17.4
Private residential neighbourhoods	49.0	34.0	17.0
HOS neighbourhoods	56.0	22.0	22.0
Public housing estate neighbourhoods	51.0	40.0	14.0

Table 4.3 Public open space provides a good alternative for families to spend holidays

	Yes (%)	Neutral (%)	No (%)
Overall response	44.6	30.8	24.6
Private residential neighbourhoods	52.0	28.0	20.0
HOS neighbourhoods	38.0	31.0	31.0
Public housing estate neighbourhoods	39.0	36.0	25.0

Table 4.4 Public open space will enhance interaction among family members

	Yes (%)	Neutral (%)	No (%)
Overall response	41.0	36.4	22.6
Private residential neighbourhoods	47.0	35.0	18.0
HOS neighbourhoods	36.0	28.0	36.0
Public housing estate neighbourhoods	39.0	41.0	20.0

Table 4.5 Public open space has created a friendlier community environment

	Yes (%)	Neutral (%)	No (%)
Overall response	41	35	24
Private residential neighbourhoods	48	33	19
HOS neighbourhoods	36	31	33
Public housing estate neighbourhoods	40	39	22

While we cannot tell the actual differences in the design and physical configuration of public open space in private and public housing neighbourhoods, one can assume that management of public areas (mostly undertaken by the public sector Housing Department) in the public housing neighbourhoods would tend to be more rigid and less customer-oriented. This brings us to the next question, how should the built environment be managed so that young people can benefit from it?

Management of public space in the built environment

From the above phenomenon, one could see that there is a need for both well-developed hardware and software infrastructure in order to get the residents and youngsters to be more committed to their own community. While ample provision of public space will suffice in terms of hardware requirements, there are a lot more considerations for the software framework. The core issue here is management of public space. The survey illustrates that in general, about 41 per cent of the responding young people find the management style of public facilities in their immediate neighbourhoods satisfactory and 20 per cent are not feeling the same (Table 4.8). In the second level analysis, the picture becomes clearer that private sector facility managers in the private residential neighbourhoods as well as private sector management contractors employed by the government taking care of the HOS neighbourhoods have done a more satisfactory job than the public sector itself. This echoes very much with findings from studies on the general level of low appreciation of management services provided by the public sector (Li and Siu, 2001).

Flexible management of such public space must be employed so that there is an 'invitation' effect for the residents to utilize public space in the first instance and then participate in the social interaction taking place on it, and hence the sense of neighbourhood will then be enforced. We have found that 48 per cent of these respondents agree that managers of public space should not control such healthy activities as cycling taking place in public areas as they tend to make the neighbourhood more lively (Table 4.6). In addition, 53 per cent of them also agree that more carnival-type activities should be held in the public space for residents' benefits (Table 4.7). Such desire for provision of more events and activities is also found in other youth studies (see Woolley *et al.*, 1999). While it will make the facilities managers' task much easier if utilization of public space and community facilities can be kept under strict control, some social/community objectives will not be served if community space management is always maintenance-oriented.

For example, Photo 4.1 shows an open space that lies between a private housing development and the shopping mall.

After this picture was taken, our research team walked five minutes to a public housing estate nearby and took another picture (Photo 4.2) of an open space in that public housing estate, which also lies between the housing towers and the shopping mall in the public housing community.

These pictures were taken five minutes apart. The contrast is very obvious.

Built environment and young people's personal development

Similar to studies elsewhere, built environment has an impact on youngsters' personal feelings and development (Gutenschwager, 1995; and Malone, 2002). In this study, close to 40 per cent of the respondents agree that the design of their community and the built environment affects their personal mood very frequently (Table 4.10), while 43.4 per cent of these youngsters regard the built environment as having an influence on their own personal development (Table 4.9). Only roughly 20 per cent of the respondents disagree with the above two notions. What is interesting from this is the fact that despite 45 per cent of these young people agreeing that such large public spaces can provide a good alternative for family members to spend their holidays together and most of these youngsters can identify a large public open space

Photo 4.1 Vibrant public open space.

Photo 4.2 Under-utilized public open space.

Table 4.6 Public open space should be managed in a more positive attitude towards youngsters' activities

	Yes (%)	Neutral (%)	No (%)
Overall response	48.0	28.0	23.2
Private residential neighbourhoods	53.0	26.0	21.0
HOS neighbourhoods	40.0	28.0	32.0
Public housing estate neighbourhoods	49.0	25.0	26.0

Table 4.7 More community-based activities such as carnivals should be arranged in public space

	Yes (%)	Neutral (%)	No (%)
Overall response	53.0	28.6	18.4
Private residential neighbourhoods	56.0	28.0	15.0
HOS neighbourhoods	39.0	35.0	25.0
Public housing estate neighbourhoods	60.0	26.0	13.0

Table 4.8 Management of facilities in the community

	Satisfied (%)	Neutral (%)	Dissatisfied (%)
Overall response	40.5	39.9	19.6
Private residential neighbourhoods	46.0	38.0	16.0
HOS neighbourhoods	49.0	30.0	21.0
Public housing estate neighbourhoods	30.0	48.0	22.0

Photo 4.3 Playground is an important outdoor classroom for children.

Table 4.9 Built environment has an impact on youngsters' personal development

	Yes(%)	Neutral(%)	No(%)
Overall response	43.4	36.5	13.1
Private residential neighbourhoods	44.0	35.0	21.0
HOS neighbourhoods	44.0	30.0	26.0
Public housing estate neighbourhoods	47.0	37.0	17.0

Table 4.10 Built environment very often affects youngsters' mood

	Yes (%)	Neutral (%)	No (%)
Overall response	39.4	38.1	22.5
Private residential neighbourhoods	43.0	36.0	22.0
HOS neighbourhoods	44.0	32.0	24.0
Public housing estate neighbourhoods	39.0	38.0	23.0

Table 4.11 Young children enjoy staying in the neighbourhood during holidays

	Yes(%)	Neutral(%)	No(%)
Overall response	26.9	35.8	37.3
Private residential neighbourhoods	29.0	33.0	38.0
HOS neighbourhoods	32.0	34.0	34.0
Public housing estate neighbourhoods	23.0	36.0	41.0

Table 4.12 Degree of participation in community events

	All(%)	1/3(%)	None(%)
Overall response	3	34	56
Private residential neighbourhoods	3	37	53
HOS neighbourhoods	3	33	58
Public housing estate neighbourhoods	3	33	58

in their neighbourhoods, only 27 per cent state that they like to stay in their neighbourhood during holidays and 37 per cent of them dislike such an idea (Table 4.11). In fact, in the preceding 12 months immediately before the interview, only 3 per cent of these youngsters participated in almost every social activity organized by the neighbourhood network, 34 per cent only participated in about 1/3 of these activities and, most alarming, 56 per cent never in the past year took part in any of these functions (Table 4.12). Most of these neighbourhood-inactive youngsters gave the reasons that they could not get a friend to go with them and most of these social activities 'were boring anyway'! This reinforces the observation above that young people do feel the potential impact of their immediate built environment on their own personal development, but there are not enough external 'incentives' to induce them to be more participatory, and this contributes to the apparent failure for them to build up 'social capital' on the network and resources from their neighbourhood community.

Sense of neighbourhood among youngsters

Social capital is defined by Coleman (1990) as a resource embodied in the relations among persons and positions that facilitate action. In other words, social capital provides different groups in the society (especially disadvantaged groups such as children) with resources, otherwise not reachable, which will form certain 'networks, norms, trust that facilitate coordination and cooperation for benefit' (Putnam, 1993: 36). Given that children have no access to other forms of capital assets, social capital accumulated in the built environment provides them with the most tangible form of network for their development. In fact, if public space cannot draw residents, especially young people, to be more socially interactive so as to develop their neighbourhood network, it is difficult to maintain and even develop a more cohesive sense of neighbourhood for social capital to be accumulated.

We measure this neighbourhood interaction by means of their degree of acquaintance with neighbours, although this should not be by any standard seen as an indication for the measurement of social capital. In our study, it is found that 10 per cent of these young people don't know any neighbour in their community and 24 per cent only know the neighbour immediately next door. Together with another 32 per cent who know only a few neighbours, we have a rather gloomy picture in this aspect (Table 4.13). These numbers show that it is difficult for us to expect young people to communicate with adults in their neighbourhoods, inside and outside of their families, when they face personal problems. Small and Supple (2001) note that the lack of a proper environment for the young people to communicate with non-parental adults will eventually drive them to explore the adulthood experiences on peer culture only, which is contingent on the culture of their own neighbourhoods. It is therefore not surprising to see that only 33 per cent of them express that being able to watch adults communicate with each other in their neighbourhoods is important to their own personal development while 46 per cent of them do not have a view on this and 21 per cent disagree with this premise at all (Table 4.14).

While in the previous observations it is found that young people in the subsidized housing neighbourhoods (i.e. the HOS neighbourhoods) tend to be rather indifferent towards their neighbourhoods, these young children, however, seem to be more socially interactive with their neighbours than their counterparts in the private and public (rental) housing neighbourhoods. In fact, 8 per cent of the HOS youngsters know almost all of their neighbours in their community compared to

Table 4.13 Degree of acquaintance with neighbours

	Know most neighbours (%)	*Know a few/ next door only* (%)	*Know no one* (%)
Overall response	18.4	56.0	10.6
Private residential neighbourhoods	15.0	59.0	11.0
HOS neighbourhoods	24.0	49.0	5.0
Public housing estate neighbourhoods	17.0	62.0	8.0

Table 4.14 Watching other adults interact with each other is important

	Yes (%)	Neutral (%)	No (%)
Overall response	33.1	45.9	21.0
Private residential neighbourhoods	35.0	45.0	21.0
HOS neighbourhoods	32.0	39.0	29.0
Public housing estate neighbourhoods	35.0	47.0	18.0

5 per cent from the public housing estates and 4 per cent from the private neighbourhood. On the down side, 5 per cent of the HOS youngsters know nobody compared to 8 per cent in public housing estates and 11 per cent in the private sector. Hence, it does not hold that young people from families on housing subsidies tend to be less community-active or even more anti-social. This observation forges a better argument for housing policies intended to mix different social groups together within a single community, such as the Moving to Opportunity in the US. This also echoes our argument for a more active exploration of the concept of 'mixed-income' housing community in the previous chapter.

Satisfaction with the physical settings in their home-based neighbourhoods

To measure young people's level of satisfaction with their neighbourhood's built environment on a much more tangible scale, we examine their responses on a number of environmental cognitions. In general, young people can accept the level of noise in their neighbourhood. It seems however, strangely enough, that HOS neighbourhoods provide the quietest environment for the youngsters rather than the private residential neighbourhoods, or than the public housing estates. The same is also true concerning management of public facilities inside the neighbourhood. This relatively satisfactory level of tranquillity found in the HOS neighbourhoods however should not be attributed to the lack of activities in the neighbourhood as there seems to be adequate facilities provided to generate resident-wide activities. Similarly, the children in the public housing neighbourhoods are the least satisfied group in terms of provision of facilities in their community, yet they find their neighbourhood most noisy among the three (Tables 4.15 and 4.16). Hence, the level of noise normally generated in a neighbourhood does not necessarily hinge on the number of children 'hanging around' in public facilities, but may be a function of a number of factors

Table 4.15 Degree of tranquillity in the community

	Satisfied (%)	Neutral (%)	Dissatisfied (%)
Overall response	55.0	25.5	19.4
Private residential neighbourhoods	59.0	23.0	18.0
HOS neighbourhoods	62.0	21.0	17.0
Public housing estate neighbourhoods	48.0	29.0	23.0

Table 4.16 Provision of facilities in the community

	Satisfied (%)	Neutral (%)	Dissatisfied (%)
Overall response	38.0	34.8	27.2
Private residential neighbourhoods	42.0	33.0	25.0
HOS neighbourhoods	40.0	29.0	31.0
Public housing estate neighbourhoods	29.0	41.0	30.0

such as design of the housing units and the overall community such as a car park. This particular aspect will need to be further examined in future research agendas.

In terms of safety in the neighbourhood, the normal perception of the correlation between public housing communities and a relatively less-safe environment seems to hold. Among the three neighbourhood categories, only the private residential neighbourhood has a satisfactory level above average and slightly beyond the 50 per cent majority threshold. It should also be noted that in the public housing estates, there are equal percentages of young people feeling satisfied with the safety level in their community as in the case of those who do not have an opinion on it (Table 4.17). This illustrates that public housing neighbourhoods have long been regarded as social welfare only and well-provided and well-managed community services similar to those found in the private housing neighbourhoods should not be dismissed as luxury.

City development and children's mobility

From above, we know that the physical environment that is constantly shaped and re-shaped by real estate development and decisions has a strong impact on children's development, among other social, personal and familial factors. The physical configuration of the city also constrains and even directs children's mobility to a large extent. Studies have shown that independent mobility is a very important learning tool for children. This is especially the case when children are growing up in the cities where neighbourhood safety is complicated by building design, traffic arrangement as well as community planning. Most of the studies and examinations on children's independent mobility (CIM) concentrate on qualitative analysis of how children carry out their activities. Despite the fact that the benefits of independent mobility with respect to child development are well documented, such mobility is still very much constrained by the urban spatial planning system created and designed by adults in our society. Apparently, our

Table 4.17 Safety in the neighbourhood

	Satisfied (%)	Neutral (%)	Dissatisfied (%)
Overall response	44.6	37.4	18.2
Private residential neighbourhoods	51.0	33.0	16.0
HOS neighbourhoods	43.0	38.0	19.0
Public housing estate neighbourhoods	40.0	40.0	20.0

city planning and urban design practices are still not factoring in children's independent mobility when formulating urban plans.

As an initiative, our team has started a project which measures parents' willingness to allow their children to carry out unsupervised activities in various cities. Among other factors, characteristics of the neighbourhood such as constant heavy traffic volume may affect the attitude of the parents towards a more liberal view on children's independent mobility. On the other hand, types of housing and perception of fear in the neighbourhood also contribute to the limitation on children's mobility. Hence, physical configuration of the neighbourhood environment accounts for an important role in affecting parents' perception of neighbourhood safety, which influences to the degree of children's independent mobility. Initially, we find that cities with more densely developed neighbourhoods with mixed uses of land, such as Chongqing and Hong Kong, tend to make more parents relatively more comfortable to allow their children to carry out unsupervised activities during the daytime. Consequently, it is necessary to examine how neighbourhood design, development density and land use pattern of the neighbourhood may impact on children's independent mobility.

Photo 4.4 Densely developed cities such as Chongqing have mixed-use activities near most of the housing communities.

Moreover, a survey was conducted by the University of Westminster in 1994 with the residents living in mixed-use neighbourhoods, and it was found that fear of crime is less and perceptions of personal safety out alone after dark are much better when compared with the UK national statistics (Pettersson, 1997: 192). Neighbourhood design that facilitates and promotes a higher degree of safety in the common area will therefore also allow a higher degree of independently mobility for children.

Our project intends to compare various cities in Asia to examine whether and how the land use settings in each of the cities may affect parents' decision to be more stringent or liberal as far as children's independent mobility is concerned. While our research is still at the very rudimentary stage, we need to point out therefore that city land development, urban planning analysis and children's mobility and their personal development also cross paths on the study of the built environment.

Chapter summary

We have seen that young people do feel that the physical land use environment in which they live and play does have an impact on their own development and even personal temperaments. They acknowledge that public space is important for their own community and they recognize that public space will stimulate family members' interaction to some extent. However, in practical terms, it seems these young people are not keen on capitalizing the benefits of the land use settings surrounding them, as noticed in their indifference towards community/neighbourhood activities and their eagerness to explore friendship with neighbours. There are certainly many reasons for it, but management and proper utilization of public space seems to be an important factor for further studies.

Overall, we have found a high concentration of responses in the 'no opinion' option in most questions. This seems to be a reflection of the high school education training in Hong Kong (and probably in some Asian cities as well) where students have not been trained to think and to question the status quo, although this trend is being reverted towards more critical thinking in these cities.

The notion of 'building a nice environment' in the context of government policy in Hong Kong almost invariably evolves around the use of environmentally friendly building materials and protection of nature. Very seldom would the government consider the correlation between the built environment and social effects. The simple analysis above shows that, for example, children in the public housing estates also aspire to have well-managed open space and facilities in their community that can be comparable to the private housing community. However, the current debate in Hong Kong is to develop a 'pragmatic' type of subsidized housing community with only minimal facilities. The argument for this approach is price. Apparently, it only makes sense to sell subsidized housing at an affordable price level when these housing estates are developed with only minimal standards, such as without a reasonable clubhouse in the estate for residents to interact in. I cannot fully comprehend this logic, but I can't emphasize more greatly that even urban land policy has a social objective of achieving a more balanced development in the society, without upsetting the main capitalist mechanism. An obvious example that we see from the survey is that quite a number of young people prefer to live in a larger community where they can have better community services. In a compact city such as Hong Kong, the government can achieve this by selling larger parcels of land to the developer or by encouraging more market-led comprehensive urban renewal schemes via speedier and easier site assembly processes. While people might argue that selling larger sites will only benefit larger developers with adequate invest-ment capital, it is always possible to break this monopolistic situation by, for exam-ple, limiting specific land auctions to only small- and medium-size companies with the hope that they will be encouraged to joint venture together, or by some other more innovative measures. This is much better than seeing single-block buildings being developed with no communal facilities, let alone public open space, to achieve the results stated above. Housing development, especially in the public sector, should not be just about building a decent shelter for the relatively lower-income groups. Housing development should also aim at building a 'home' for these families within a community that can foster a good sense of belonging for everyone in it.

More importantly, government should set up channels and mechanisms to 'invite' young people to voice their needs and views on the policy relating to the built environment. We should be aware that young people have no direct vested interest or political agenda on the built environmental issues and, hence, they will not tend to express themselves actively. They need to be guided and stimulated to express their views, for instance through more learning activities, such as the YouthPower projects in the US or the Growing Up in the Cities workshops in various countries. Unless we maintain that young people belong to the future and have no place in the current decision-making process, this is a new area for the public sector to step into.

Note

1 According to Sampson, 'routine activities' perspective has been well applied in the field of criminology to study the correlation between the physical environment and motivation of crimes.

5 Market behaviour and real estate

L.H. Li

I am interested in behavioural economics when I get flyers from real estate development projects (for example, Photos 5.1 and 5.2 on pages 64 and 65) near our campus which emphasized that the project was prime because it was near to the University of Hong Kong (or did until recently when these advertisements actually specified that it is because of the new MTR station at HKU). At first, I did not think anything of such statements. Then I realized something was a bit off. I understand the importance for some real estate projects of being near to traditional famous primary or secondary schools, as location makes the household part of the specific school-net that will help gain entrance to such desirable schools. But university's entrance consideration is a whole different story. As far as I know, universities in Hong Kong do not really consider the applicant's home address when recruiting students. If being near to the university does not really account for an advantage for secondary school children, why do these advertisements still emphasize that the project is near a scholarly institution? Would universities emit a certain aura to the atmosphere that will make people nearby more elegant and scholarly? Is the university neighbourhood safer? (It will be interesting to know the actual statistics, but, from my own experience, our conference room on campus has lost three overhead projectors in only two months!) If the answers to these are no, then I think people are being led to believe that the psychological impact of a good neighbourhood with the presence of a higher educational institution could be true, although it is also interesting to note that there are studies showing potential negative impacts on the housing market for being close to higher educational institutions (Vandegrift *et al.*, 2012; Kashian and Rockwell, 2013)! This certainly echoes with our discussions above on the general perception of the importance of the immediate neighbourhood to our children's development. The following photos were taken by the author from the promotional materials that belonged to a new housing development near the university. The marketing team was certainly well-aware of this importance of a good neighbourhood to homebuyers!

More importantly, basic economic teachings are built on the assumption that the market and people are rational so that rational predictions can be made when applying economic principles. But, on a daily basis, how often are we acting rationally? How often do we regret our decisions made on impulse rather than carefully calculated assessments of the pros and cons before writing the cheque?

Photo 5.1 Advertisement of a new housing project with an emphasis that it only takes five minutes to walk to the University of Hong Kong.

Why did some developers choose to sell their new projects in the middle of the night? In any case, studying behavioural impact on the property market is an interesting development as the real estate market is infamous for its inefficient nature as an asset market and, hence, human nature plays a much larger role in its performance. In the following chapter, we will briefly look at some issues that show an interesting combination of psychology and real estate studies that may have important implications for the government as a regulatory body and for the ordinary homebuyers or private developers.

Introduction

The real estate market has long been known for its inefficient nature (Fu and Ng, 2001; Dunse *et al.*, 2010). One manifestation of such inefficiency is the problematic

Photo 5.2 The same project highlighting the rich 'academic atmosphere' for being near to the University of Hong Kong, which could affect the good students around!

information flow in the market mechanism. Because most real estate markets lack a central clearing house for changes in information to be reflected in market prices and because of the heterogeneous nature of housing products (with the exception of REITs), no single participant in the market can gain an understanding of the full and complete picture without incurring substantial transaction costs. Nevertheless, the majority of real estate studies are still founded on the neoclassical economic theories that assume consumers are rational and are capable of making informed choices in order to maximize their utility and wealth (Gibler and Nelson, 2003). Traditional approaches of property studies therefore mainly rely on economic modelling and quantitative techniques to analyze the property market (Ball, 1998). These approaches are closely related to investment analysis so they can also be called a finance paradigm. These approaches have dominated the field of property studies for a long time (Diaz III, 1999). Based on these assumptions, economic activities in the property market can be predicted within reason without considering the problem that consumers do not always act in a rational way, and most agents in the market do not possess adequate information to do so. Consequently, different approaches to supplement these conventional rational approaches (but not to replace them) are called for. One of these supplementary perspectives is the behavioural approach. In recent decades, the study of how behavioural science works in economic activities has gained more and more momentum. Camerer and Loewenstein (2004: 3) explain that '...behavioural economics is the conviction that increasing the realism of the psychological underpinnings of economic analysis will improve the field of economics on its own terms...'.

Given the highly inefficient real estate market and the vast numbers of sellers and buyers operating in it, it is absolutely conceivable that application of behavioural economics can improve our understanding of how the real estate market works and hence increase the accuracy of real estate market analysis as well as market appraisal. Adair *et al.* (1996), in their study of the participant behaviour in the Belfast housing market, note that real estate valuers actually have a different view on principal determinants of property values than the sellers themselves. Diaz III and Wolverton (1998) also find strong evidence pointing to the connection between behavioural pattern and appraisal smoothing. Genesove and Mayer (2004) apply a Loss-Aversion model to examine seller behaviour in the Boston housing market and find that sellers whose unit's expected selling price falls below their original purchase price set an asking price that exceeds the market level. Based on their model, they conclude that

> ...the underlying fundamentals of housing market cycles are cyclical than they seem. Since at the trough of the cycles, loss-aversion and equity constraints lead many sellers to set relatively high reservation prices, buyers valuations must actually be more volatile than the observed transaction prices...
>
> (Genesove and Mayer, 2004: 652)

Therefore, a thorough understanding of how individuals react and behave when faced with different situations is an essential step for a better understanding of the how the real estate market would react to these situations. We use three most common situations, namely market valuation, market information interpretation and market perception, to illustrate this.

Real estate research and market/individual behaviour

Valuation

Property valuation as a discipline is a combination of both arts and science, in theory and in practice as information selection by valuers is an essential part of the process whichever model is being undertaken. The selection process by definition involves personal decision-making by the valuers or the private individuals involved. In the valuation process, considerable amounts of information have to be faced by the valuers as well as the individuals, for example, the general market economic data, the specific characteristics of the property and the statutory documents, etc. In this respect, one cannot ignore the potential psychological impact on the appraisal decision. Psychological phenomena associated with these information-processing strategies may affect the final conclusion based on the available information. The final valuation figures may be affected by the behavioural phenomena.

Over the years, a growing number of papers have concentrated on this area of behavioural property valuation studies. Examples can be found from literature on valuation judgements in terms of differential reference points; transaction feedback; client feedback and client influence (Diaz III and Hansz, 2001; Havard, 2001; Gallimore and Wolverton, 1997; Levy and Schuck, 1999). Findings from these and other published research projects have made contributions to the aspects of property market pricing and the construction of real estate indices. Arising from these studies, analysts and academia have begun to look at the impact of behaviour of participants in the property market including consumers, lenders, brokers, investors, developers and landowners. The importance of human behaviour to the valuation discipline is supported by the increasing number of behavioural property research published in the leading refereed journals.

In this respect, we need to turn to the recent development in Behavioural Economics for more inspiration. Berry (2001: 50) remarks that 'Behavioural economics examine the classic theories about how people – and businesses – respond to price changes and other phenomena...by plugging in formulas that capture more closely how individuals really behave...'. In general, all human beings go through two modes of analysis in their own mind. The first mode is the rational choice: choices are slower, more controlled, rule-based and reasoned. In the second one, choices are based on perception and intuition; they are made quickly, effortlessly, automatically and may not be reasoned. The Nobel Laureate in Economics, Professor Vernon Smith points out that there are five major areas where psychology contributes to a better understanding of economics (Smith, 2005). Among these five propositions, he states that markets cannot be rational if agents are not fully rational in the particular sense. In addition, no agents can achieve socially optimal ends without a comprehensive understanding of the whole, as well as their individual parts, implemented by deliberate action. Because of this, one cannot test the rationality of individual decisions by asking for subject responses to choice problems to discover how they 'reason'. Market information, even delivered in a completely honest manner, is subject to interpretation by individuals, which leads to very different results due to differences in personal experiences and knowledge level in the market. These differences therefore further affect the quality and magnitude of input into different valuation models that may or may not give a comprehensive reading of the actual market situation. So it becomes interesting to understand the extent to which this irrational reasoning exemplifies in our property market.

Given the highly inefficient nature of the property market, it is not unreasonable to expect that professionally trained valuers will have a very different view on the attributes affecting property values from buyer/seller's viewpoint. If the differences cover a wide range of factors and lead to differences in the relative importance of these factors, then it is a major source of disagreement in the assessment property (rental) value derived from even an established market mechanism.

Table 5.1 Analysis of the Belfast detached-house market

Attributes	Buyers' ranking	Valuers' ranking
Neighbourhood condition	1	1
House size	2	5
Plot size	6	20
Types of neighbouring houses	22	6
On-site parking	7	21
Layout	10	23
Travel time to work	14	47
Non-residential uses	27	7
Number of reception rooms	16	8
Modern kitchen	20	12
Modern bathroom	21	13
Exterior condition	8	19

Source: Adair, Berry and McGreal (1996) (p. 30).

Adair *et al.* (1996), carry out an interesting study of how professional valuers and private individuals place different rankings on various attributes affecting property values. In their study of the participant behaviour in the various sub-sectors in the Belfast housing market, they note that the valuer group attaches higher scores to and places greater emphasis on environmental/locational attributes relative to the buyer group. Based on this finding, they remark that 'Accepting this hypothesis, the key question to emerge is whether such difference is reflected in a significant variation between the price set by negotiation and interaction in the market and the valuation of residential property by the professional practitioner...' (Adair *et al.*, 1996: 31). Table 5.1 is one of the sub-markets they examine and it is obvious that with the exception of the factor 'Neighbourhood Condition', valuers and buyers differ in a lot of other categories and in some cases quite substantially. For example, while most buyers in their study regard plot size and on-site parking as important, valuers do not quite think so. On the other hand, valuers place high emphasis on the types of neighbouring houses and the element of non-residential uses while buyers would not have that same level of regard. If two models are built based on these two rankings, it is very likely that two sets of very different values will emerge within the same market environment, but due to very different personal judgements.

Interpreting market information

Sometimes, the divergence in market opinion stems from the environment in which different groups of people interpret market information (even the same set) differently, irrespective of what their personal experiences and knowledge level are. This potential bias of view derived from the so-called market information was first developed in the inspirational work by Tversky and Kahneman (1974), in which they developed a number of attributes that would lead to this bias. Among all the attributes, this chapter concentrates on the factor known as the recency effect. In short, new information arriving at the open market carries mixed directions and interpretation. When such kinds of information are received, there will be a tendency for greater weight to be attached to the most recent piece of information, this is the recency effect. Two different persons receiving the same set of information about the market, but in a very different order may arrive at different conclusions.

Wolverton and Gallimore (1999) conducted the first research in this stream that involved over 200 commercial and residential valuers in a postal survey in the early 1990s. To test the recency impact, respondents were given a 50 per cent confidence interval of the market value of a property on a per square foot basis. Respondents were segmented into two groups by presenting two sequences of comparable data that the respondents could use to adjust their initial confidence intervals. The comparables presented were in one of the two following sequences: two positive comparables followed by two negative comparables or two negative comparables followed by two positive comparables. The results were that the group receiving the positive comparables last was more confident in their value estimate than the group receiving the negative comparables last. The findings of this study suggest that the order in which valuers process evidence may influence their conclusions. Valuers seem to give greater credence to information most recently considered. Differences in information sequence, for example the order in which comparable sales are examined, may evoke different interpretations of the same set of evidence. Therefore, it may lead to different value conclusions.

In 2006, one of my undergraduate students in the BSc. in Surveying programme at the Hong Kong University conducted a similar test with a much smaller sample base when writing his final year dissertation. Structured interviews with ten professional General Practice surveyors were carried out. These ten surveyors were all in the 30–40 age group, with an average of six years' valuation experience in Hong Kong. The average number of valuation tasks performed per annum was 48. Again, this student confirmed the findings of Gallimore. It is therefore possible that even under a complete competitive market, experienced valuers receiving information in a certain manner may have a very different view on the attributes of value component than the other players in the market, leading to a very different result in assessment judgements, such as identifying the reference assessment or making adjustment to different variables. Ever since this interesting dissertation, I have applied the same experiment in my postgraduate classes in Hong Kong and in many cities in Mainland China. Most of the time, I get the same result as Gallimore, and students are always amazed how their views will swing when receiving information in that manner.

Market perception[1]

In this section, we will examine a particular aspect of this behavioural approach in the real estate research known as the 'Framing Effect' and explore how this effect impacts on consumers' and hence the overall market perception of the housing market movements.

Framing effect is related to media reporting behaviour of market performances. The most common form of mass media is usually manifested in the 'news'. News is defined as 'any report of an event that happened or was disclosed within the previous 24 hours and treats an issue of ongoing concern' (Jamieson and Campbell, 1992). From this, we observe that news has two important characteristics: (1) it consists of recent information (usually within 24 hours); and (2) it covers ongoing concerns of the general public. Hence, it has been regarded that news is a more powerful way to shape the public perception than other mass media because most people accept the message from news as incontestably reflecting reality (Harris, 2009). News is also a core source of information from which the general public obtain data and facts for their own decision-making processes. This is especially important when the news is about specific sectors of the economy where not every average citizen has equal access to a comprehensive set of data and information. Real estate market is one of these specific economic sectors.

First of all, we need to understand that there is a close relationship between mass media and psychological influence. When we interact with media/news reports, there are many psychological processes occurring, including cognitive and emotional processing of information. Cognitive process refers to the 'thought process' that includes paying attention to some information presented by the media and neglecting other information; understanding the information presented by the media; interpreting them by our mind and experiences; and finally remembering the information (Harris, 2009). This aspect has received a lot of attention in the research arena (Lang and Shapiro, 1991; Shapiro, 1991; Hawkins *et al.*, 1987). For emotional process, the content of the media can influence the audience's feeling and even judgement on the subject. For instance, it has been shown that media can apply mood management to regulate the sentiments of the target audience (Knobloch-Westerwick and Alter, 2006).

How do the messages conveyed by mass media shape market perception? In psychology, '*perception*' is defined as 'the process by which an organism attains awareness or understanding of its environment by organizing and interpreting sensory information' (Nadel, 2003). Thus, based on this psychological definition of perception, we depict real estate market perception as 'the process by which individuals understand the real estate market environment by organizing and interpreting real estate information'.

Following this definition, market perception in the real estate economy is individuals' understanding of the performance (including risk and return prospects) in the real estate market after they have received, absorbed, interpreted and, potentially, acted on such information. In addition, market perception is closely associated with the behaviour of market players and it will eventually drive the 'aggregated' market behaviour when most people form similar perceptions. Individuals' perceptions of the market will guide their behaviour. Therefore, when market players begin to observe 'signs' of economic downturns, consumers' perception will be affected significantly and they will become pessimistic towards the future. Consequently, they will become eager to sell their properties or defer their buying plan because of such pereption (Wu *et al.*, 2009). With the exception of a few senior professionals with good personal connections with the developers and the authorities, most people in the real estate market search for these 'signs' via market news. We therefore observe that the relationship between real estate market perception and news media is very close. Based on this, we will develop our analytical framework with the help of an understanding of the framing effect.

Framing effect

Framing effect has recently gained popularity in the analysis of how opinions or perceptions shape public policy. This can range from government's defence for military action (Perla Jr., 2011) to unhealthy food choices (Kees, 2011) to presentation of a fiscal bonus (Lozza *et al.*, 2010).

Framing effect, explained from a psychological perspective, is a powerful way to alter the attitude of the audience. According to de Vreese *et al.* (2011), research on framing effects can be categorized into the studies of 'belief importance', which examines the relative perceived importance of different aspects of an issue; and the studies of 'belief content', which analyses the additional and new contents brought about by framing. Sociologists divide the frame construction into micro-level and macro-level (Scheufele and Tewksbury, 2007). Micro-level frame construction describes how individuals use their own frame to organize their impression and information in order to formulate their own interpretation about the world (Scheufele and Tewksbury, 2007). Macro-level frame construction, sometime called *agenda setting*, describes how journalists and reporters present the information in a pre-designed schema that resonates with the schema among their audiences (Reese, 2007).

More interestingly, framing effects may not impose the same magnitude or even direction of impact on everyone in the audience equally. Groups within an audience receiving the same 'framed' information may end up making different choices, due to some specific differences in personal characteristics among these groups. Framing effect has been shown to affect specific gender under certain circumstances (Fujimoto and Park, 2010). Dunegan (2010) finds that students with higher GPA scores (and hence better academic attainments) tend to be more easily affected by framing agents than their counterparts with lower GPA scores. On the surface of such findings, it seems to be contradictory to the common belief that higher academic attainments provide a better shield for the persons to fence off biased information. Nevertheless, Dunegan explains that students with higher GPA scores also exhibited higher level of sensitivity towards incoming information and, as a result, they tend to 'have been looking beyond the objective value of the information provided, and reflecting on the implied theme of the framed scenarios' (Dunegan, 2010: 244).

Gibler and Nelson (2003) suggest that making decisions in the property market is a complex process that involves considering information from various sectors in the economy and sources. Most homebuyers/renters therefore tend to seek external help from such sources as real estate market news and real estate agents.

Their review of this information-processing framework in the property market suggests that the general public, as opposed to seasoned professionals with good connections, tends to adopt the 'shaped' intuition without any further consideration. Therefore, most buyers in the market are expected to be more easily influenced by the framing effects. Jin (2009) carries out an experiment in America and his finding supports this argument. He studies how people change their perception of the property market in the US after reading his 'framed' news articles. People who have read the optimistically framed news article tend to be more optimistic towards the property market and vice versa.

Research design

My student, Mr. Alex Fong, and I did a small experiment in November 2010 in Hong Kong to explore this aspect of market perception. The targets in this controlled experiment were 111 university students from two universities in Hong Kong. We acknowledge that the sample size is relatively small, but nonetheless acceptable. In terms of educational background, the students are more or less the same. Among the 111 participants, 63 participants were studying for or had studied the Bachelor of Science in Surveying[2] as their undergraduate programme and 48 students did not have such background at the time of this experiment. The core variable between these two groups is the benefit of an academic background in real estate studies. The difference in perception between these two groups of participants is analysed to answer the research question set out above. Among the 63 participants with real estate academic knowledge, 18 were first-year students, 21 were second-year students, 18 were final-year students (in a three-year study programme) and 6 were recent graduates with no more than one year of working experience at the time of writing.

Some demographical attributes are also measured, including gender and nationality. Among all the participants, 51 are male (46 per cent) and 60 are female (54 per cent). In terms of nationality, 89 are Hong Kong permanent residents while 22 are non-Hong Kong residents. None of the participants were homeowners or had been personally involved in property transactions at the time of the experiment.

To facilitate the analysis, all participants are divided into two major groups: A and B. Group A is made up of participants without a real estate/surveying educational background; Group B is made up of participants with a real estate/surveying educational background.

Since the core objective of this research study is to analyse and distinguish the relative impact of positively and negatively framed news on participants with and without a real estate/surveying educational background, the framing effect is designed to compare two major groups of participants under the opposite directions of framed news.

Before conducting the experiment, all participants had to answer the first part of the questionnaire concerning their initial market perception. The questions in the questionnaire are the same for all participants. Next, they were divided into two main groups according to the framed article they were about to read. Hence,

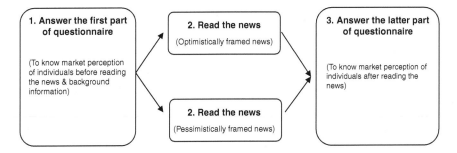

Figure 5.1 Experiment procedure summary.

in each main group, there would be both participants with and without a real estate/surveying educational background. After reading their prescribed set of framed news articles, participants from these two groups were required to answer the latter part of the questionnaire, which aimed to find out their market perception after receiving the framed information. The whole experiment flow is summarized in Figure 5.1.

To analyse the problem more robustly, we have to ensure that the two hypothetical news articles should share the same facts about the Hong Kong real estate market so that the difference in market perception is only due to the change of the frame in the news articles. Those facts shared between the two hypothetical news articles are listed below:

- Property price increased 1.1 per cent in October.
- Three supporting factors contributed to the Hong Kong property market, namely: a substantial flow of 'hot money' into the economy, a low interest rate, and an under-supply of flats in the recent years.
- There has been a 42 per cent surge in housing prices since the beginning of 2009.
- Property transactions were 10,900 units this month compared to 11,700 units the previous month.
- In 2010, the residential price index was 1.88 times of the GDP per capita index.

To enhance the credibility of the newspapers, these facts mentioned in the hypothetical news articles were real and extracted from two real estate news articles published in a local newspaper in Hong Kong.[3]

The contents of these two real articles were then re-worded and framed to suit the purpose of this analysis, namely one set was optimistically framed and the other one was pessimistically framed. The example below illustrates the manipulation process.

- Pessimistically framed: Under the *cooling* measures, the increasing trend slowed; property price increases only 1.1 per cent, therefore there is a *pessimistic* outlook for the market.

- Optimistically framed: Even under the *stabilizing* measures, the increasing trend continued; Property Price still increased 1.1 per cent, therefore there is an *optimistic* outlook for the market.

These examples share the same basic fact: the property price increased 1.1 per cent during the reported period, but the two articles have been framed with the use of optimistic words and pessimistic words respectively. For example, 'cooling' and 'slowed' are pessimistic words while 'stabilizing' and 'increasing' are optimistic words.

Empirical results

Before analysing the framing effect, we need to examine the perception of the participants as a control. Through a series of questions in the survey and without going into the details of the technical analysis (which can be found in the original paper) in this section, we find that sentiment of all participants about the market was very similar in the 'pre-framing' stage. Hence, all participants were on equal footing as far as market perception was concerned before the framing effect impacted on them in this experiment.

After the framing experiment, we notice that there is a tendency for such perception to change in some groups of the participants. First of all the perception of non-real estate students was easily enhanced or depressed by positively or negatively framed news, depending on which group of 'framed' news they read. This change of perception was equally applicable to their view on both the current and future market direction. As result, non-real estate students in this group who were given positively framed news tended to recommend their friends to buy property after reading the news, while other non-real estate students who were given negatively framed news tended to advise otherwise. The impact of framing that helped to swing their opinion was very obvious in this group.

On the other hand, real estate students tended not to be influenced by the framing effect as far as the immediate market performance was concerned in the experiment. Real estate students who read positively framed news did not react significantly more positively than their counterparts who read the negatively framed news. It was very likely that they might not have relied entirely on the information given by the news article. Their exposure to the current market situation via their real estate knowledge received in the academic programme, or the initial contact with the market for those who just graduated might have helped them make a better judgement of the current market situation. However, when it comes to the perception of the market performance in the future, their current exposure to the real estate education may not have accommodated them with such knowledge, and they fell back to the same information-processing behaviour adopted by the non-real estate students. Hence, students who read the negatively framed news were significantly pessimistic about the future, and that led to their tendency of not recommending their friends to become property-owners in the near future.

It is clear that students without real estate academic knowledge are relatively easily affected by the framing effect of news articles and this result matches with the result of Jin (2009). It seems that students without the benefit of real estate academic knowledge rely on their own knowledge of the market acquired elsewhere and direct intuition when making responding to 'framed' news. Consequently, the framed news article is able to manipulate and shape the reaction of readers (Scheufele and Tewksbury, 2007). An optimistic market view is formed after they have read an optimistically framed news article, and vice versa.

Some participants were interviewed after the experiment and shared with the research team how their decision-making process was formed during the experiment. Their responses support our explanation. The dialogue between one of the participants is shown below:

> Team: Did you encounter any difficulties in comprehending the real estate news?
>
> Student A: '...In general, I can understand the content of the news. However, I can't quite understand the technical terms, such as affordability...'
>
> Team: Can you share your decision-making process during the experiment?
>
> Student A: '...I don't have a clear idea about Hong Kong property market...instead of analyzing the content of news, I focus on the words: optimistic outlook, upward trend for making decisions...'

This group of students agree that making decisions in the property market is a cognitively demanding activity so they rely on their intuition, which was shaped by the framed news in this experiment.

On the other hand, when we look at the group with real estate academic knowledge, it seems they were not as easily affected by the framing effect, as far as the current market state is concerned during the experiment. However, their market perception of the future market performance and market risk perception was affected by the framed news in the experiment. It therefore seems likely that students possessing real estate academic knowledge are able to fence off framing effect by making logical assumptions based on their academic knowledge and training in the field. They can make easy connections with what is going on in the market irrespective of the wordings they were presented with in the news article. However, when it comes to the future prospect of the market, including risk perception of the real estate market, there are too many variables for them to decipher in order to make rational decisions. In addition, this kind of practical forecasting may not have been covered in their course. For example, government policies may change from time to time and market supply and demand data are not usually part of the academic syllabus. Moreover, reading into the future changes in the market is more likely to be dependent on practical and professional training that they do not receive in an academic programme but that will be part of their future work in the field. In this case, they are at equal par with the other group without such academic knowledge. Again, reflection from one participant in this group confirms our analysis here:

> Team: Did you encounter any difficulties in comprehending the real estate news?
> Student B: '...I can understand the content of the news. I don't feel any difficulties in comprehending the news...'
> Team: Can you share your decision-making process during the experiment?
> Student B: '...for current property market, I don't really pay attention to those emotional words...I just take the figures and statistics as reference.... However, for future property market...I don't have a clear idea because I need to consider many perspectives, such as changing economic environment, changing government policies.... It's difficult and, I choose to believe the prediction in the news.'

The findings suggest that the framing effect of real estate news can affect consumers' market perception. According to the empirical results, students and recent graduates with real estate academic knowledge perform better in their ability to fence off framing effects than students without real estate academic knowledge. But this ability seems to be limited only to the current market situation. For a longer-term prospect into the future, practical knowledge and personal experience in the market remain utmost important in assisting good decision-making, in addition to the fact that market variables in the future are too many to control.

Chapter summary

What we have seen in this chapter is a glimpse of how we, as an ordinary house-buyer or as a seasoned property professional, may be affected by sentiment when making a real estate decision. Invariably, the role of information plays a very important role in this research direction and one of the more interesting foci is the study of framing effect in the real estate market. Framing effect, explained from a psychological perspective, is a powerful way of changing the attitude of an individual and is formed by utilizing his own belief. When individuals receive a framed message or information, the weighting of various attributes in this belief will change. Jin (2009) carried out an experiment in America and his finding showed how people changed their perception of the property market in the US after reading the 'framed' news articles. People who had read an optimistically framed news article tended to be more optimistic towards to the property market and vice versa.

By understanding more about how information and perception may affect real estate decisions; this research angle can help the government and different players in the market to realize the importance of getting a more comprehensive picture of the situation before making policy action or investment decisions. Maybe next time when we hear that a market survey was conducted and X per cent of the people agreed on a certain issue, we may step back and think about how that question was asked in the first place before siding with this opinion. After all, whoever controls the flow of information controls market sentiments!

Notes

1 This section is adapted from the paper by the author published in the *Journal of Real Estate Practice and Education*. The full reference of this paper is: Li, L.H. (2012) 'Real estate education, professional training, and market bias: a behavioral study in Hong Kong', *Journal of Real Estate Practice and Education*, 15 (2): 129–51. Online. Available: <http://search.proquest.com/docview/1315923915?accountid=14548>. The author would like to thank the American Real Estate Society for granting the permission to reproduce part of the paper here in this chapter.

2 Surveying is a British-based profession that is basically about the real estate and construction market. According to the description of the undergraduate programme, the BSc in Surveying offered by the Department of Real Estate and Construction, the University of Hong Kong, the course is 'an interdisciplinary academic program fostering rigorous critical inquiry into the economics, financial, legal, and managerial aspects of real estate and construction...' (source: <http://fac.arch.hku.hk/index.asp>).

3 These two pieces of news articles are: Chung, S. 'Residential Property is Getting More Dangerous: Concrete Analysis', *South China Morning Post*, 25 August 2010; and Leung, P. and Li, S. 'John Tsang Still Sees Bubble Risk, Though Flat Price Rises are Slowing', *South China Morning Post*, 27 April 2010.

6 Built environment and senior citizens

L.H. Li and Tiffany Chung

We have examined the effect of the physical environment on children in Chapter 4. In this chapter, we elaborate how the impact might be felt on a very different sector of our society, namely senior citizens. Similar to children, senior citizens tend to spend a lot of their time in their immediate home environment. Unlike children, some senior citizens have stronger financial independence, meaning their choice of the living environment is more flexible. Again, we would like to use this opportunity to illustrate that real estate research can be applied to determine the relationship between the built environment and the level of happiness of senior citizens and how the major determinants of the built environment may influence this level of happiness among senior citizens in Hong Kong. But again, we need to reiterate that 'happiness' is a multi-faceted phenomenon and we by no means want to conclude that the environmental factors discussed in this chapter will definitely contribute unconditionally to elevate the degree of happiness among senior citizens anywhere.

Introduction

According to the Hong Kong Life Tables conducted by the Census and Statistics Department in 2010, the population in Hong Kong is experiencing a noteworthy increase in longevity. Over the past 38 years, life expectancy for males has risen from 67.8 to 79.8 years, while that for females has increased from 75.3 to 86.1 years. The life expectancy of men in Hong Kong is projected to increase to 83.7 years and of women to 90.1 years by 2039.

The elderly population in Hong Kong is surging at an unprecedented speed. According to the population projection conducted by the Census and Statistics Department of the Hong Kong government in 2006, the population of people in the 65+ age group in Hong Kong will reach 28 per cent of the total population, or 2.5 million in 2039. Meanwhile, the total fertility rate (TFR) has shown a drastic decline without sign of recovery in the near future. With the combined effects of improved longevity and long-lasting below-replacement fertility, the ageing population has significantly accelerated in Hong Kong. The population is expected to remain on an aging trend for the foreseeable future. Hong Kong is going through a striking demographic transformation, which will inevitably give rise to new challenges and demands.

Facing the aging population, there is increasing demand for the provision of elderly housing. Since a variety of age-related ailments and constraints may arise as an individual gets older, the demand of senior citizens for housing arrangements may vary a lot from the non-elderly population. At the same time, with the progress of social development, the provision of mere physical accommodations may not be able to fulfil the changing needs of the elderly people.

Caring for the senior citizens has always been a major concern of society and they were one of the first few target groups to benefit from welfare policies in the new administration in Hong Kong in July 2012. Therefore, it is of paramount importance to construct a desirable living environment in which the special needs of the elderly population can be adequately catered for so as to maintain a sustainable future for Hong Kong.

Importance of planning for elderly housing

In many Asian countries and cities, such as Japan, Korea and Hong Kong, adult children bear the responsibility of taking care of their aging parents under the traditional culture. Therefore, multi-generational living used to be a common practice.

However, the traditional living arrangement of the multi-generational family has been declining in recent decades. David and Alfred (2002) explain that the housing and accommodation needs of the elderly people can be attributed to several prevailing social trends. These involve a surging demand of the elderly people for separate living from their adult children, thereby increasing the desire for privacy and a decline in multi-generational sharing, especially given the small living units that prevail in some densely developed cities, such as Hong Kong. Therefore, such new demand patterns of the elderly housing should be taken into account in developing senior housing projects.

It may be argued that in places where the cost of accommodation is high and where property is jointly possessed by the family, multi-generational families still persist. Nevertheless, with prosperity, improved job mobility, multiple income earners and more choices for housing, nuclear households generally dominate over co-residence in most of the cities around the world (Brink, 1997).

As there is an increasing number of elderly people living by themselves due to the breakups of extended nuclear families, the number of households consisting of only elderly members increases accordingly. Therefore, the demand for community support of the elderly population increases as well.

The current situation of housing of senior citizens in Hong Kong

According to the 2006 Population By-census, there were a total of 852,796 elderly people aged 65 or over in Hong Kong. In terms of the proportion of the senior citizens in the overall population, its percentage reached 12.4 per cent. In 2006, there were 594,730 domestic households with at least one elderly person, constituting 26.7 per cent of the total domestic households in Hong Kong.

For the types of housing these senior citizens reside in, 41.1 per cent (315,242) of the elderly people lived in public rental housing, while 16.6 per cent (127,193) lived in subsidized sale flats. Among the 41.3 per cent (316,861) senior citizens living in private permanent housing, 15.0 per cent (47,509) were the tenants of their accommodations in 2006. It was estimated that about 1.0 per cent (7,817) elderly people lived in temporary structures including roof-top structures and temporary huts where the living condition were unsatisfactory in the same survey.

Owing to the decline of the traditional multi-generational families, merely 53.4 per cent of the elderly people lived with their children (30.4 per cent lived with spouse and children and 23.1 per cent lived with children only) in 2006. In addition, 21.2 per cent lived with spouse only and 11.6 per cent lived alone.

Despite the fact that senior citizens possess a higher priority in housing allocation through various welfare housing schemes in Hong Kong, they still have to wait for several years to obtain a public housing unit. Besides, the demand for the housing units provided by such semi-public housing development organization as the Hong Kong Housing Society is also higher than the current supply. This reveals that the provision of elderly housing is inadequate to cater for the demand in the society though a variety of assistances have been provided.

As researches have shown that higher income is usually related to higher educational attainment, the recent improvement in educational attainment of the younger cohort of senior citizens is expected to raise the proportion of middle-class senior citizens in the future. According to the Census and Statistics Department of Hong Kong in 2006, the proportion of senior citizens with no schooling or only pre-primary education dropped from 43.7 per cent in 1996 to 35.8 per cent in 2006. At the same time, the proportion of people who aged 15 and above with secondary or higher education attainment increased from 67.9 per cent in 1996 to 74.6 per cent in 2006. Therefore, educational attainment of the future cohort of elderly people is expected to have even greater improvement. As a result, it is conceivable that the proportion of middle–class senior citizens will increase further in the future. Therefore, the demand of this group should be carefully considered.

Future retirees with a higher educational level will possess higher expectation for their later life. Life styles, identity and choices become the key concept of post-modernity in the community. Factors influencing housing demand of senior citizens include a wide spectrum of aspects such as housing aspiration, housing mobility, sociological factors, housing affordability and housing consumption pattern. Senior housing therefore should not be just viewed as physical shelter for the aged to spend the last stage of their lives.

Significance of home for senior citizens

As stated by Brink (1997), housing is a defining factor for quality of life. Although longevity is generally regarded as desirable, it may no longer be pleasing for an aged individual who possesses a low quality of life. This stresses the importance of housing in the life cycle of an individual. Brink (1997) further explains that the daily routines of people, especially senior citizens, occur in the settlement in which their homes are located. Therefore, the influence of housing on the quality of life is particularly significant for senior citizens.

The Aged & Community Services Australia (2004) also affirms that home has special significance for senior citizens. This idea can be further elaborated in the results of a study conducted by Davison *et al.* (1993) for the sake of understanding the importance of housing and neighbourhood for the elderly. The result of the study articulates that home is a place which senior citizens are familiar with and where they feel that their lives are under self-control. Following this premise, the better the quality of the home, the higher the level of self-control these senior citizens may have over their lives. In recent decades, economic, social and political policies of different countries all seek to promote aging in a supportive environment. Therefore, the built environment that is favourable to the living of senior citizens should be investigated.

Major determinants of built environment in happiness of senior citizens

'Evidence suggests that there is a link between suitable housing infrastructure and well-being of rural people' (Hillier *et al.*, 2002). This notion is reinforced by Guster (2002) who states that the physical and psychological well-being of elderly people is intrinsically related to the built environment of their accommodations. Similarly, an extensive literature and studies support that aspects of the built environment significantly influence the life satisfaction of the elders.

As pointed out by Phillips (2000), the role of environment can be divided into internal and external aspects in planning and designing housing units for senior citizens. Internal environment involves the design of the home, access, maintenance and architectural aspects; while external environment involves open spaces, recreational facilities, shops, welfare and medical services. Wright and Kloos (2007) reinstate that the housing environment can be conceptualized as existing at the apartment, neighbourhood and the community levels. A multi-dimensional construct of built environment can be formed by combining the factors in the three levels together.

The following factors are in general regarded as important environmental factors that will impact on senior citizens. Some of them will also be applied in the study of Hong Kong to be illustrated below:

1   Availability and accessibility of community support (Streib *et al.*, 1986; Brink, 1997)
2   Accessibility to transportation (Wireman and Sebastain, 1986; Brink, 1997)
3   Household density (Mitchell, 1971; Galle *et al.*, 1972; Bogdonoff *et al.*, 1991; Pastalen, 1990; Heumann and Boldy, 1993)
4   Family and social relationships (Brink, 1997)

5   Living arrangement
6   Community identity (Kichen and Roche, 1987; Sidnell, 1995; Heywood
     et al., 2001)
7   Housing tenure type (Gurney and Means, 1993; Brink, 1997)

Real estate research and senior citizens

As the aim of this chapter is to investigate the factors contributing to a desirable living environment in which senior citizens in Hong Kong could achieve a higher level of happiness, the external and internal conditions of the built environment in which the elderly people in Hong Kong are living will be covered. It is hoped that the discussion in this study can contribute towards the discussion on how urban planning and housing policies can help to create a more desirable built environment for the senior citizens in the society. Since the focus of this study is the built environment, other non-environmental factors, notably health, personal and familial, contributing to the happiness of the elderly will not be fully covered. In the following, we will introduce a study through which the correlation between some built environmental factors and the well-being of senior citizens will be assessed. The well-being of senior citizens is proxied by a measurement of the degree of happiness.

Owing to the limited time and resources, the sample size is only 250 in this study, which we acknowledge is far from satisfactory. The eligible respondents for the questionnaire are people who were aged 65 or above at the time of our interview (November–December 2012) and were not living in senior housing or were under medical care during that period. The questionnaire consists of 3 parts with a total of 30 questions:

Part 1 (General information)

The purpose of this part is to collect the background information, including age, gender, religion status, educational attainment, employment status and monthly income of the respondents. The intention of setting questions concerning demographic characteristics is to collect data for the non-environmental factors that may likely contribute to the happiness level of the elderly people.

Part 2 (Conditions of the built environment)

In this part, questions are included mainly to collect data for the independent variables of the built environment in the statistical model. These built environment factors are based on literature review and the existing situation in Hong Kong. Besides, some questions in relation to non-environmental factors are also involved.

Part 3 (Happiness level)

This part is constructed to measure the happiness level, which represents the dependent variable in the statistical model. To this end, a basket consisting 12 questions is

Photo 6.1 Parks near the housing community provide a platform for interaction among senior citizens.

Photo 6.2 The clubhouse in private housing communities is usually mostly utilized by senior citizens during the daytime.

used as the instrument for measuring the happiness of the respondents. Besides, it is conceivable that the level of optimism will directly affect the happiness of an individual. Therefore, a question in relation to this factor is also included in this part.

Measuring happiness

According to the World Database of Happiness (Veenhoven, 2005), there are currently 1,291 variants in the acceptable measurement of happiness. In previous studies and research pertaining to the psychological condition of an individual, the level of happiness is generally quantified as a happiness index with a specific measurement tool based on the unique circumstances in each case. Therefore, the dependent variable in the analytical model in this study is defined as the happiness index for measurement purposes.

In the absence of a measurement tool with a universally acceptable standard in this discipline, an instrument adopted by Mroczek and Kolarz (1998), known as the Affect Balance Scale, is applied in measuring the happiness level of senior citizens in Hong Kong in this discussion. The happiness measurement is a self-report process which comprises of 12 questions (A-L) about the frequency of different feelings of the respondents in the past 30 days immediately before the survey. The computation formula is $(G+H+I+J+K+L)-(A+B+C+D+E+F)$ with a verbal scale of 5 for each item. Together, the 12 questions form a basket measuring the happiness level of the respondents with a minimum score of -24 and a maximum score of 24. A higher score indicates higher level of happiness, and vice versa.

This instrument has undergone substantive psychometric work and exhibited comparable internal consistency (Evans *et al.*, 2002). In 2005, it was applied to measure the happiness of the elderly in Spain in a similar study. Therefore, this instrument is regarded as appropriate for measuring the happiness of the respondents in this discussion.

Independent variables of built environment

Types of accommodation

To increase the richness of the data, the types of accommodation of the respondents are further divided into eight categories based on the types of housing and tenure. The independent variables concerning the types of accommodation are summarized in Table 6.1.

Built environment of neighbourhood

To facilitate the operation of the model, the availability and accessibility of the relevant facilities are quantified as the travel time from the accommodation of the respondents to the nearest location with an ordinal scale of 1 to 5. Besides, the usage of the amenities by the elderly is also incorporated into the model to increase the comprehensiveness of the analysis.

Table 6.1 Summary of variables: type of accommodation

Independent variables	Description	Utilization of variables
OP_S	Owned private housing (single block)	Dummy variable: 1 represents
OP_E	Owned private housing (comprehensive type)	the type of housing is of the specified type of the
OP_H	Owned private housing (house)	respondent, 0 otherwise.
RP_S	Rental private housing (single block)	All zero represents other
RP_E	Rental private housing (comprehensive type)	types of housing.
RP_H	Rental private housing (house)	
HOS	Housing under Home Ownership Scheme	
PHE	Public housing estate	
OWNER	The possession of ownership of the accommodation	Dummy variable: 1 represents the possession of ownership of the accommodation, 0 otherwise.

Apart from the public amenity facilities available in the community, a club-house in the private housing estate may also greatly contribute to the built environment of the neighbourhood, especially for the elderly people who possess a relatively low mobility. A clubhouse in Hong Kong can provide the residents with a comfortable living environment and leisure opportunities in close proximity to their homes. In Hong Kong, the majority of comprehensive type of private housing possesses a private clubhouse in which well-served recreational amenities are available and highly accessible. In view of the importance and prevalence of clubhouse in Hong Kong, the usage of clubhouse of the elders is also defined as an independent variable in the equation to increase the comprehensiveness of this study.

In order to examine the significance of the effect of facilities on the happiness of the elderly people more comprehensively, the usages of the corresponding facilities are incorporated into the model as well. To measure this independent variable, the usage is quantified as the average number of times the respondents visit and utilize the facilities per month.

In order to measure the accessibility of public transportation, travelling time from the accommodation to the nearest MTR station is used as a proxy with an ordinal scale of 1 to 5.

Table 6.2 summarizes the description and utilization of the independent variables concerning the built environment of neighbourhood.

Physical environment of accommodation

Other than the observable conditions of the built environment, the foreseeable changes in the living environment may also influence the perception and psychological well-being of the elderly people. Accordingly, both the existing conditions

Table 6.2 Summary of variables: built environment of neighbourhood

Independent variables	Description	Utilization of variables
DLIB	Travelling time from the accommodation to the nearest library	In ordinal scale (1–5): 1 represents the least travelling time while 5 represents the longest. Below shows the basis of assigning the rating to the data in travelling time (in minutes):
DCOM	Travelling time from the accommodation to the nearest community centre	

Travelling time (in minutes)	Rating
0–9	1
10–19	2
20–29	3
30–44	4
45 or above	5

Independent variables	Description	Utilization of variables
DCC	Travelling time from the accommodation to the nearest civic centre	
DSPORT	Travelling time from the accommodation to the nearest sports facilities	
DMEDI	Travelling time from the accommodation to the nearest medical facilities	
DOPEN	Travelling time from the accommodation to the nearest open area	
DMTR	Travelling time from the accommodation to the nearest MTR station	
UCLUB	Usage of clubhouse	Dummy variable: 1 represents the elderly use the clubhouse, 0 otherwise
ULIB	Usage of library	In ordinal scale (1–5): 1 represents the least usage while 5 represents the greatest. Below shows the basis of assigning the rating to the data in number of times visiting the facilities per month (in average):
UCOM	Usage of community centre	
UCC	Usage of civic centre	
USPORT	Usage of sports facilities	
UOPEN	Usage of open area	

Number of times visiting per month	Rating
0–1	1
2–3	2
4–5	3
6–9	4
10 or above	5

and anticipated changes of the physical environment that surrounds the accommodation of the respondent are taken into consideration in this study.

Existing conditions of physical environment

The effects of household density and the number of people living together on the happiness of the elderly will be tested in this study. Besides, living density, which is calculated by dividing the usable floor area by number of people living in the accommodation, is also incorporated into the statistical model to facilitate the study of the effect of household density.

Additional variables concerning the quality of the living environment are also added into the model. In Hong Kong, floor level and views of the accommodation are undoubtedly regarded as some of the important determinants in the quality of the living environment. Generally, the majority of people prefer higher-floor living because of the availability of superior view, better air quality and less noise in higher-floor level. According to a study conducted by Yuen and Yeh (2011), the average highest preferred floor level is approximately 29.3 for Hong Kong. Meanwhile, the variation in flat price can also reflect the preference of the general population. In Hong Kong, the prices and rentals of units with higher-floor level and superior views are proportionately higher than the others. Therefore, the floor level, the availabilities of different views (such as mountain view and sea view) are incorporated into the model to examine their effects on the happiness of the elderly people.

Added to the above, the physical conditions and maintenance status of the building are also important to the elderly people. As mentioned above, elderly people are the vulnerable group in the society. The majority of them possess a low mobility with different kinds of impairments. Therefore, their specific needs concerning the building safety should be catered for so that they are able to live independently with a sense of security and dignity. In measuring the physical conditions and maintenance status of the building, building age and the requirement of renovation plan are used as proxy.

Anticipated change in the physical environment

Since the 1980s, massive urban redevelopment projects with different scales were launched by developers in Hong Kong. In a redevelopment project, residents originally living in the targeted redevelopment area as well as the immediate neighbourhood are considerably affected. Generally, a significant change in the built environment will be inevitable (Chui, 2000). Therefore, a dummy variable regarding the existence of redevelopment plan within the foreseeable future is also incorporated in the statistical model in order for a better understanding of how imminent redevelopment affects our respondents.

Non-environmental independent variables

Demographic characteristics

Demographic characteristics which may affect the level of happiness of the senior citizens mainly include age, gender, religious commitment, educational level, monthly income, employment status and health status (Baldassare *et al.*, 1984; Mroczek and Kolarz, 1998; Hyde, 2005).

Living arrangement

The extent of family support received by senior citizens is significantly affected by co-residence (Phillips and Chan, 2002). In general, the living arrangement can be classified into three types, namely living alone, living with relatives, and living with others. In this study, we therefore assess how such living arrangement may impact on the livelihood of senior citizens. Though it is not directly an environmental variable, the outcomes may impact on various aspects of housing and community design principles.

Family, social and neighbourhood relationships

Support from family and friends are imperative to senior citizens (Brink, 1997). The family, social and neighbourhood relationships are basically the outer-ring of the living arrangement outlined above. Again, the outcomes may also have impacts on community design that facilitates this networking arrangement.

Level of optimism

Last but not least, the personality and perception of an individual undoubtedly influences his or her happiness level even if other factors are all kept constant. In the other words, the level of optimism of the respondents may contribute considerably to their psychological well-being. In this case, we try to insert this variable to estimate such effect.

General model

Assuming that the multiple regression model is in linear form, a dynamic equation is shown below:

Happiness Index (denoted as HI)= f (Type of Accommodation, Built Environment of Neighbourhood, Physical Environment of Accommodation, Non-environmental Factors). When this is converted into a statistical formula, it will look like the followings:

$$HI = a + b_1RP\_S + c_1DMTR + c_2USPORT + d_1RENO + d_2REDEV + e_1OPTI + e_2ASSIST + e_3SOCIAL + e_4FAMILY + e_5EDU + f$$

where

HI is the happiness index computed by Mroczek and Kolarz (1998) Affect Balance Scale;

a is the constant term;

b_1 is the partial coefficient of the variables in the type of accommodation;

c_1 and c_2 are the partial coefficients of their respective variables in the built environment of neighbourhood;

d_1 and d_2 are the partial coefficients of their respective variables in the physical environment of accommodation;

e_1, e_2, e_3, e_4 and e_5 are the partial coefficients of their respective variables in the non-environmental factors;

RP_S is the dummy variable representing rental private housing (single block);

DMTR is the travelling time from the accommodation to the nearest MTR station;

USPORT is the usage of sports facilities;

RENO is the dummy variable representing the requirement of renovation for the building;

REDEV is the dummy variable representing the existence of redevelopment plan within the coming three years;

OPTI is the level of optimism;

ASSIST is the dummy variable representing the requirement for assistance in daily life;

SOCIAL is the social relationship;

FAMILY is the family relationship;

EDU is the educational attainment;

f is the stochastic error term.

Sub-models

In view of the relatively large number of independent variables in this study, the data set is further divided into subsets according to the type of accommodation so as to provide more specific investigations for different parties in the society. As a result, two sub-models examining the impact of built environment on the happiness of the senior citizens living in private housing and public housing estates are developed respectively.

Public housing estates

The sub-model for public housing estates is constructed through the same model selection procedures. By incorporating the remaining variables after backward elimination, a dynamic equation is shown below:

$$HI = a + b_1DMEDI + b_2USPORT + c_1AGE + c_2OTHERS + c_3FAMILY + c_4ASSIST + c_5SOCIAL + c_6OPTI + f$$

where

HI is the happiness index computed by Mroczek and Kolarz (1998) Affect Balance Scale;

a is the constant term;

b_1 and b_2 are the partial coefficients of their respective variables in the built environment of neighbourhood;

c_1, c_2, c_3, c_4, c_5 and c_6 are the partial coefficients of their respective variables in the non-environmental factors;

DMEDI is the travelling time from the accommodation to the nearest medical facilities;

USPORT is the usage of sport facilities;

AGE is the age of the respondent;

OTHERS is the dummy variable representing living with people other than relatives;

OPTI is the level of optimism;

FAMILY is the family relationship;

ASSIST is the dummy variable representing the requirement for assistance in daily life;

SOCIAL is the social relationship;

f is the stochastic error term.

Private housing

The sub-model for private housing is constructed in the similar manner. The dynamic equation is shown below:

$$HI = a + b_1 DLIB + b_2 USPORT + b_3 DOPEN + c_1 RENO + c_2 REDEV + d_1 OPTI + d_2 FAMILY + d_3 ASSIST + d_4 EDU + d_5 SOCIAL + f$$

where

HI is the happiness index computed by Mroczek and Kolarz (1998) Affect Balance Scale;

a is the constant term;

b_1, b_2 and b_3 are the partial coefficients of their respective variables in the built environment of neighbourhood;

c_1 and c_2 are the partial coefficients of their respective variables in the physical environment of accommodation;

d_1, d_2, d_3, d_4 and d_5 are the partial coefficients of their respective variables in the non-environmental factors;

DLIB is the travelling time from the accommodation to the nearest library;

USPORT is the usage of sport facilities;

DOPEN is the travelling time from the accommodation to the nearest open area;

RENO is the dummy variable representing the requirement of renovation for the building;

REDEV is the dummy variable representing the existence of redevelopment plan within the coming three years;

OPTI is the level of optimism;

FAMILY is the family relationship;

ASSIST is the dummy variable representing the requirement for assistance in daily life;

EDU is the educational attainment;

SOCIAL is the social relationship;

f is the stochastic error term.

Table 6.3 Distribution of geographic location of respondents

Location	Frequency	%	% by 2006 Population By-census
Kowloon	76	41.3	39.3
New Territories	70	38.0	39.4
Hong Kong Island	38	20.7	21.3
Total	184	100.0	100.0

Descriptive data

There are in total 250 questionnaires in which 184 samples are valid. With respect to the geographic location of the respondents, 41.3 per cent of the respondents live in Kowloon. Table 6.3 details the geographical distribution of the respondents. Comparing with the statistics provided by 2006 Population By-census, the data set used in this study is representative of the distribution of population of age 65 or above in Hong Kong.

For the gender distribution (Figure 6.1), it is quite even. 87 (47.3 per cent) are male and 97 (52.7 per cent) are female.

Regarding the age distribution (Figure 6.2), the mean age is 73.6 and the standard deviation is 6.8. The maximum age is 92 while the minimum is 65. Overall speaking, 62 (34 per cent) respondents are between the ages of 65 and 69.

Among the 184 valid respondents, 89 (48.4 per cent) are religious while 95 (51.6 per cent) are not (Figure 6.3).

With regard to the educational attainment (Figure 6.4), 64 (35 per cent) of the respondents have attained secondary or sixth-form level of education; 57 (31 per cent) and 47 (26 per cent) are illiterate and possess primary level respectively. Less than 10 per cent (16) of them have attained post-secondary education.

As to the employment status (Figure 6.5), a majority (87 per cent) of the respondents are retired while the remaining is not.

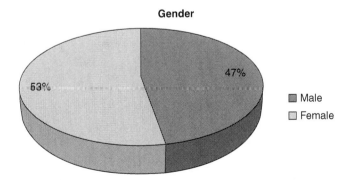

Figure 6.1 Frequency distribution of gender.

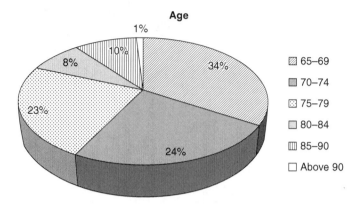

Figure 6.2 Frequency distribution of age.

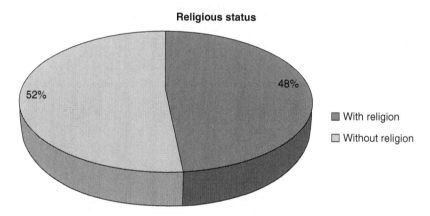

Figure 6.3 Frequency distribution of religious status.

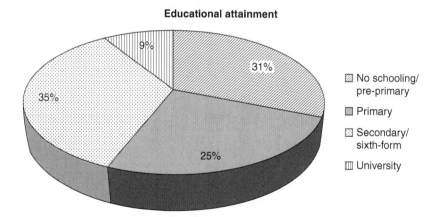

Figure 6.4 Frequency distribution of educational attainment.

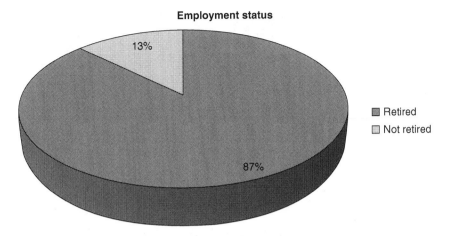

Figure 6.5 Frequency distribution of employment status.

In terms of the financial situation (Figure 6.6), 38 per cent (70) of the respondents have a monthly income less than HK$2,000. Another 33 per cent (60) possess an income between HK$2,000 and HK$3,999 per month.

Concerning the type of accommodation (Figure 6.7), 38 per cent of respondents live in single-block building, which they own. Another 27 per cent live in public housing estates. Besides, 10 per cent live in subsidized housing programme known as the Home Ownership Scheme (HOS). Only 2 per cent of them live in the comprehensive type of private rental housing. Meanwhile, none of them live in private rental houses (detached or semi-detached, which are the very top end of accommodation in Hong Kong). With reference to the General Household

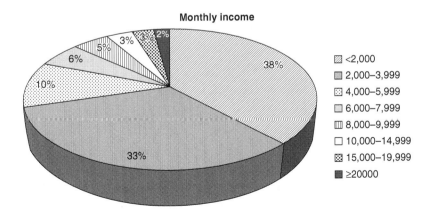

Figure 6.6 Frequency distribution of monthly income.

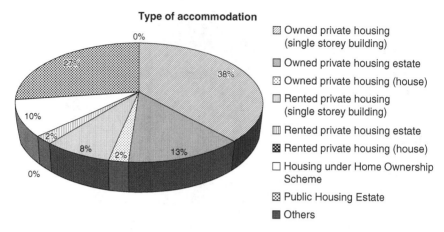

Figure 6.7 Frequency distribution of type of accommodation.

Survey in Hong Kong (C&SD, 2008), among the elderly people who are not institutionalized, 37 per cent and 18 per cent of them live in public housing estates and subsidized sale flats respectively. The remaining 45 per cent reside in various types of private permanent housing. Therefore, the distribution of type of accommodation in this data set is comparable to that in the senior citizens in Hong Kong.

For the living arrangement (Figure 6.8), the majority of the respondents (79 per cent) live with their relatives, such as their spouse and children. Besides, 14 per cent of them live alone. In the data set, only 7 per cent of the elderly people live with people other than their relatives.

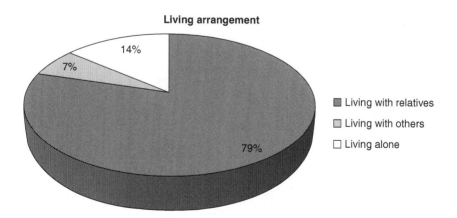

Figure 6.8 Frequency distribution of living arrangement.

Discussions

Environmental factors

Types of accommodation

We find that senior citizens in our sample who are tenants and are residing in private single-block building are relatively less happy compared to others who are in other housing arrangements. This is consistent with the expectation that elderly people living in rental housing may feel less secure about their accommodation because uncertainty exists whenever the lease expires. They may be forced to move due to upward adjustment of the rent or the discretion of the landlord when the contract ends. It is evident that a stable life is preferred by the majority of people, especially the elderly who possess a lower physical mobility. In addition, single-blocked residential buildings usually lack communal facilities such as a clubhouse or other amenities due to the limitation on the plot. While this may not be a major problem for younger people who can travel to other places for physical exercises or social events quite easily, this limits the choice of life style for senior citizens. Thus, the lack of security of tenure coupled with a lack of facilities exert a negative impact on the senior citizens living in this environment. As a result, it is conceivable that living in the private rental single-block building poses a negative effect on the psychological well-being of the elderly. Meanwhile, it is surprising that senior citizens who are property owners are not found to be significantly happier. In other words, the possession of homeownership does not provide an extra contentment to the elderly people in Hong Kong. This is in opposition to the general notion and previous literatures which suggest that homeownership has a positive impact on the happiness of people as it provides a representative of status and a sense of superiority (Gurney and Means, 1993). However, we need to caution readers that this could be due to the limitation in data. Financial data on mortgage re-payment on the residential flats these respondents own are essential for a better understanding of why this ownership is not significant. But this kind of data is usually difficult to obtain from senior citizens by survey.

In addition, senior citizens living in public housing estates and HOS are not significantly happier or 'unhappier' than other groups in our model. Moreover, we cannot find any significant difference between the two sub-models, namely public and private housing types. In other words, the elderly people are indifferent between residing in public housing estate and in private housing in terms of their happiness level. One possible explanation is that clear boundaries for different types of housing are usually undistinguishable in the compact city of Hong Kong. In other words, the residents living in different types of housing actually share a common built environment of the immediate neighbourhood in which they enjoy the same community facilities and transportation provided by the government. In addition, 'private housing' embraces a very wide range of social-economic groups who sometimes may not be more financially well-off than their counterparts in the public housing community. Consequently, the effect of different types of housing is relatively low in Hong Kong.

Built environment of neighbourhood

Among the 13 independent variables related to the built environment of neigh-bourhood, only distance to the underground railway (MTR) station, is found to be influential. Apparently, being near to a MTR station contributes positively to the level of happiness among senior citizens in Hong Kong and vice versa. This result reaffirms the idea of Wireman and Sebastian (1986) that public transportation is one of the major factors that have to be considered when planning for elderly residential communities as it influences social interaction, and in turn the psycho-logical well-being of the older people.

In the sub-model for public housing estates, it is also found that elderly resi-dents in public housing estates become less happy as the distance from their accommodation to the nearest public medical facilities increases. In the other words, the farther they need to travel to medical care from home, the less happy they are. This finding is in line with the expectation and echoes with the previous literatures and studies that emphasize the ideas of 'care in the community' and 'ageing in place' (Fisk, 1986; Ontario Ministry of Community and Social Service, Canada, 1989; Bogdonoff *et al.*, 1991; Pastalen, 1990; Heumann and Boldy, 1993), and the importance of community health services to maintain health and a lower morbidity of the elderly people (Phillips, 2000). Besides, it is also worth noticing that the absolute value of this factor in the statistical outcome is relatively high. This reflects that the availability and accessibility of medical facilities contribute quite significantly to the happiness level of the elderly people living in the public housing estates. In contrast, this factor is insignificant in the sub-model for private housing residents. The reason may be that the residents of private hous-ing who may possess a higher financial ability prefer to use private medical services, if needed. Or, they may have better transportation mode, such as private car or taxi, which neutralizes the problem of distance. Therefore, the availability and accessibility of public medical facilities in the community are unimportant to them. This again, warrants a more in-depth analysis in the future.

In the sub-model for private housing, it is found that elderly people living in a private accommodation farther away from the open area are less happy, and senior citizens who use sports facilities more frequently are happier. This finding reinforces the idea that housing environment must support social interaction so that the senior citizens can acquire self-fulfilment and life-satisfaction (Rosenberg, 1970; Chui, 2000). Besides, the findings also support the study of Streib *et al.* (1986) who stress the importance of availability and proximity of social and recreational facilities in the living environment of the elderly. Once again, the interplay of maximizing land resources for housing development in Hong Kong and the value of open space/park is observed here.

Physical environment of accommodation

We also find that elderly people living in a building in which renovation is required are less happy. This reveals that poor physical conditions and maintenance status of the building have negative impact on the psychological well-being of the elderly.

Such negative impact may come in the physical damage arising from noise and financial damage of having to contribute to the renovation and higher management costs. This result is in line with the expectation that building safety is imperative to the elderly group who are likely to possess a lower mobility and are limited by various kinds of impairments. It is therefore natural to deduct that they can enjoy a more joyful life in a well-maintained building in which they are able to live independently with security and dignity.

Interestingly enough, it is also found in this study that the existence of a redevelopment plan of the building these respondents are living in and the immediate neighbourhood in the foreseeable future is found to exert a positive impact on the happiness of the elderly. This result contradicts from popular belief that elderly people will probably be reluctant to move away from their original accommodations because of the community identity and the familiar environment (Sidnell, 1995). Besides, it also contradicts with the idea of ageing-in-place which advocates allowing the elderly people to stay in the locality that they are familiar with. This warrants a more comprehensive analysis with a larger sample size. In the absence of these conditions, we can only speculate that elderly people may wish to move to a place that is more manageable, accessible and suitable for them than in a run-down neighbourhood (Heywood *et al.*, 2001; Kichen and Roche, 1987). Another cause of this phenomenon may be that the compensation available for the homeowners affected in the redevelopment area is relatively high in Hong Kong, especially when public authority is involved in the redevelopment scheme. Therefore, residents living in the dilapidated and obsolete buildings may be glad to accept the compensation or reallocation arrangement and move to a new accommodation in which the conditions are better.

Non-environmental factors

In all the three models, it is found that social and family relationships are major determinants affecting the happiness of the elderly people. Besides, 'perception' of the senior citizen has great impact on his or her psychological well-being. Meanwhile, elderly people who require assistance in their daily life are less happy.

Chapter summary

Once again, we have demonstrated in this chapter that the study of real estate can be conducted in a setting that is very much geared towards social aspects where the outcome does not have to be confined to monetary analyses of price movement, investment return or investment portfolio. We cannot reiterate enough that urban society is built on a foundation of physical environment which is more often than not incidental to a number of real estate and land use policies and decisions. As such, all other sub-sectors in our urban society will have to interact with these real estate and land use decisions one way or the other. While the focus of this study is on 'happiness level' of senior citizens in Hong Kong, the following real estate- and environment-related issues have also been shown to be relevant.

Stake-holders and policy-makers in these areas certainly can have a better understanding of how they impact on the happiness level of the senior citizen population from various actions they make:

1   *Planning for transportation*
    Firstly, the importance of public transportation to senior citizens is confirmed from the abovementioned results. Therefore, the government should examine and evaluate the planning for vehicular transportation, pedestrian road design as well as urban infrastructure in a comprehensive manner so as to enhance the physical mobility of the elderly residents in the community. For example, the impact of being near to MTR is very conspicuous, as the underground railway company, the Mass Transit Railway Corporation of Hong Kong, provides preferential fares to senior citizens such as a flat rate of two Hong Kong dollars (around US 28 cents) on certain days of the week. This enhances the reliance of the senior citizens on MTR services.

2   *Provisions of medical and community facilities*
    In this study, the result reveals that the availabilities and accessibilities of certain community facilities exert impacts on the well-being of the elderly in Hong Kong. For the elderly residents of the public housing estate, public medical services are essential. Therefore, medical and health care services should be adequately provided in convenient locations near to the public housing estates in order to cater for the needs of the elderly residents.

    From the results, the sports facilities and open area are found to be essential for the elders residing in private permanent housing. In congruence with the idea of ageing-in-place, this implies that sufficient and accessible recreational facilities and open area which encourage social interactions and contacts between neighbours of all ages should be available in the community so that the senior citizens would not feel being segregated from the society. For instance, more parks and elderly fitness stations with facilities such as bench steppers, back strengthening and calf stretch should be built in the community, especially in the districts where the senior citizens is high.

    Meanwhile, those community services and facilities should be integrated with one another in a coordinated and comprehensive way so as to accommodate the differential needs of the elders in the community. To achieve these, a joint effort of various welfare sector and relevant government departments are required. Therefore, the government should collaborate with different sectors in planning the built environment of elderly housing.

    Besides, the government should also encourage and facilitate private developers to supply integrated elderly housing in which care and community services to the elderly residents are considerately provided. One of the possible approaches is to regulate the development through town planning and zoning. Another method is to apply public policy tools such as granting density bonus (Hong Kong Housing Society, 2004), which permits extra development density to offset the profits lost as a result of providing facilities tailor-made for the elders. In fact, it is an incentive scheme prevailing in countries such as the United States to serve public purposes. However, its feasibility and practicability in Hong Kong should be thoroughly considered.

3   *Renovation plan*

In view of the importance of the maintenance status of building to the elderly residents, renovation and improvement works should be conducted in the dilapidated buildings in a more efficient and professional way. Government-led effort should be channelled into areas where there is higher proportion of senior residents.

Concerning the homeowners of private permanent housing, supports for renovation should be given to those living in dilapidated flats. With response to the specific needs of the elders whose physical abilities may be deteriorated, the government should encourage them to renovate the buildings with universal design in particular (Hong Kong Housing Society, 2004). This can enable them to live independently regardless of the changes in physical conditions. On the one hand, the government can provide financial assistance that covers part of the expenses to the low-income elderly homeowners. It is recommended that the extent of subsidies to be considered according to different financial abilities of the homeowners. On the other hand, renovation with universal design should be promoted, together with technical support, through various media in the old districts.

In terms of the public housing estates, Hong Kong Housing Authority (HKHA) has, in fact, endorsed the 'Estate Improvement Scheme' in early 2010. The aim of this scheme is to renovate the living environment of the public housing estates to a sustainable community with tenants of different age groups. Ping Shek Estate, a 40-year-old estate in Kowloon East, was chosen as the target in the pilot scheme in the course of redevelopment (see Photos 6.3 and 6.4). This redevelopment project started in early 2011 and is expected to complete by 2014. In the project, the external facades and internal structures of the buildings are renovated in order to ensure the building safety. Meanwhile, recreational amenities especially designed for the aged tenants are also added. Specifically, some shops are converted into a multi-purpose activity centre for the tenants to socialize and join various activities organized by different parties. Furthermore, the scheme also features the barrier-free access to increase the mobility of the elders and disabled in the community. Following this pilot project, the feasibility and efficacy of the renovation works under this scheme should be reviewed comprehensively and used as a reference for renovation in other estates in the future.

4   *Redevelopment plan*

In this study, one of the surprising results is that redevelopment brings about positive impact on the affected elderly residents. As mentioned previously, this may be attributed to the satisfactory compensation and rehousing arrangement for the affected tenants in Hong Kong. Besides, some of the elderly people may prefer to move to a place that is more manageable, accessible and suitable for them so that they can live independently with dignity. In considering this, redevelopment or rehabilitation should be reviewed in the obsolete

Photo 6.3 Ping Shek Estate after redevelopment, with facilities such as restaurant and barrier-free accessibility for the disabled.

Photo 6.4 Ping Shek Estate after redevelopment, with better-placed community facilities.

urban area so as to create a community that can cater for the specific needs of the senior residents. It is worth noticing that this idea contradicts some arguments forged by some pressure groups and political parties that redevelopment is not preferred by senior citizens in the affected neighbourhood. However, this study attempts to discuss the issue from a different perspective based on the empirical results. Meanwhile, as we cautioned above, more in-depth analysis with a larger sample base should be considered in the future.

In a redevelopment plan, considerations in economic, physical and social aspects should be taken into account for the provision of elderly housing. Regarding the economic aspect, different housing types should be included in the community for the elderly people with differential demands and affordability so that the potential buyers can be captured.

In view of the relationship between transportation and psychological well-being of the elders found in this study, the government should take this determinant into consideration in deciding the location for new public housing projects. Nevertheless, financial consideration may be a crucial barrier to locate the public or subsidized housing in the prime area that is near to MTR station and other public transport. Given the limited land resources, there may be other pressing demands for the use in a more cost-effective manner. Therefore, a balance should be stricken in determining the location.

Concerning the social issue, the rehousing arrangement for the affected elderly residents should be carefully considered in order to minimize the influence brought to them. Ideally, the elderly tenants can be rehoused within the same district or in a proximal locality so that they are able to preserve their social networks and emotional attachment in the familiar community. In addition, the abovementioned medical and community facilities should also be included in the redevelopment in order to construct a community with care. According to the integrated planning approach implemented by Elderly Commission (EC) of Hong Kong, which was set up to provide recommendations concerning elderly services, the community care for the elderly should be enhanced by stepping up inter-generational communications. Therefore, the amenities should be designed in a way that facilitates the interactions between people from different age groups.

5   *Housing policy*

The result in this study indicates that senior citizens renting private single-block buildings are less happy. As discussed before, one of the possible reasons is that they may conceive living in rental private housing as less stable, coupled with the lack of amenities in these singled-block buildings. In view of this, the government should provide more subsidized public housing units for the low-income elderly so that their waiting time can be shortened. Currently, there are approximately 7,000 elderly applicants waiting for the allocation despite the fact that their average waiting time is lower than that for the general applicants.

7 Housing choice and community attachment[1]

L.H. Li

'No man is an island'. Almost everybody lives in a community environment, one way or the other. As much as people can, they try to reside in a community of their own choice. This choice is made to a certain extent according to the attachment people have towards that neighbourhood and the physical environment. The extent of attachment residents feel towards their community and how this attachment affects their housing choice are measured in this chapter. We set out to analyze the factors affecting residents' attachment to their housing community in Hong Kong based on a conceptual framework of 'Community Quotient' (CQ). By adopting the Analytic Hierarchy Process to measure the appropriate weighting of factors regarding the attachment level among residents, we hope to contribute to the discussion of why people move to (or stay in) a certain housing community in Hong Kong.

Apart from financial reasons, such as making a profit from the appreciation of the capital value of their houses, we recognize people's desire to be attached to a certain community due to the latter's image and what it stands for, even in a small city such as Hong Kong. Thus, the connection between choice of residence and community attachment is a relevant study. As Brehm *et al.* (2004) note, most of the research focus concerning community attachment has been placed on personal and social connections, while little has been done on connections with the natural and even the physical environment. This chapter therefore fills the gap by examining such a relationship.

Community in context

The importance of examining this topic has been noted by Bryant who asserts that 'today, there is a great variety of community activities that seek to influence economic and socio-cultural activities and to contribute to the resolution of problems or impacts related to economic development' (Bryant, 1999: 70). The study of community therefore 'provides empirical investigations and descriptions of the way of life of people in particular settlements or localities' (Davies and Herbert, 1993: 4). In a more commonly held view, community is perceived as a social system containing differentiated, interlinking subsystems which operate through intricate linkages with extra-community systems (Edwards and Jones, 1976).

Community is further defined as a group of people who reside in a specific local-ity and who exercise some degree of local autonomy in organizing their social life in such a way that they can, from that locality base, satisfy the full range of their daily needs (Edwards and Jones, 1976: 12).

Simply put, a community is composed of four basic components, namely, people, geographical space, social interaction, and a common tie. Geographical space is shaped by the built structures in the neighbourhood, and very often, these built structures are housing properties. In this chapter, we provide a connection between these four elements by examining the social interaction and common tie among people in a community, and how this feeling of community attachment affects their choice of neighbourhood in Hong Kong.

Community attachment can have different meanings depending on different contexts. In general, it refers to how people feel and react towards others and the space in their living environment. This general view seemed to be shared by most scholars interested in this field (Karsada and Janowitz 1974; Beggs *et al.*, 1996; Goudy 1990; Theodori, 2000; Brehm, *et al.*, 2004). As such, it reflects the level of positive bonding or association among individuals within some physical space, as well as between individuals and their physical environment. Therefore, community attachment is to a large extent geared towards the sense of satisfac-tion one has about his/her own neighbourhood.

This sense of satisfaction with one's neighbourhood is in turn dependent on a number of attributes that enhance one's feelings towards the people around and to the environment within the community (Goodman and Hankin, 1984). Fried (1984: 62) further elaborates this sense of satisfaction by stating that, 'On empir-ical grounds, satisfaction remains a core indicator of attachment, as do a number of attitudinal and behavioral measures that may have only a tenuous relationship to a deep sense of home, of a profound local commitment, or a sense of belonging and stability'.

Community attachment and housing choice

Researchers have long been studying the relationship between residential mobil-ity and community attachment (Fredland, 1974; Rossi, 1980; Porell 1982). From these studies, I generate the following factors and analyze their relevance with the examination of community attachment and housing choice.

Neighbourhood ecological aspect

Rossi (1980) notes from his survey that complaints made against the neighbourhood environment positively correlate with mobility intentions. Therefore, neighbour-hood characteristics may influence the rate of movement. Guest and Lee (1983) also find that physical environment plays a role in community identification as well as community sentiment.

Neighbourhood environment may be indirectly related to neighbourhood safety. This is because improving the quality of neighbourhood environmental

characteristics will increase residents' concern over the appearance of the neighbourhood and the kind of people who live in their community, which in turn
enhances their perceived level of neighbourhood safety (Baba and Austin, 1989).
Residents' perception towards safety therefore exerts an impact on social integration within the community. Skogan (1987) suggests that fear, in conjunction with
other factors, can stimulate more rapid neighbourhood decline which includes the
weakening of informal social control and even more seriously, withdrawal from
community life.

Image and identity

Fredland (1974) states that perception of class identity in a community by residents
is highly significant in determining moving intentions. This perception can be
enhanced by participation in formal and social community activities. Formal
community activity participation means involvement in neighbourhood organiza-
tions such as owners' committee, whereas social activities are more leisure-oriented
events. This correlation between formal/informal gatherings and sense of neighbourhood has been empirically tested by Karsada and Janowitz (1974). They show
that length of residence is positively related to individual local friendships, community sentiment, and participation in local affairs.

Measuring community attachment in Hong Kong

To define the term 'community' in a small city such as Hong Kong may be
considered a challenge. Boundaries, except for the external walls of private housing estates, are blurred given the compact environment. Communities in this city
are therefore usually referred to as specific housing estates. Areas beyond the
gates therefore become an administrative district as defined by the government.[2]
Nevertheless, within this small city, residents' mobility is relatively high. This is
partly because of the continuous property market boom from the mid-1980s to the
mid-1990s which provided many property owners with an adequate supply of
capital from the sale proceeds of their first home for them to choose and trade up
in the market.

In this chapter, we intend to examine the extent to which this mobility reflects
residents' own perception of a particular housing community. As such, we examine
the correlation between people's housing choice and community attachment using
a standard for measuring community attachment. We apply the analytical framework by adapting the concept of Community Quotient as a means of measurement.

Community quotient is built on the notion of social capital. Social capital is
defined by Coleman (1990) as a resource embodied in the relations among persons
and positions that facilitate interaction. In other words, social capital provides
resources to different groups in the society, which will form certain 'networks,
norms, trust that facilitate coordination, and cooperation for the people's benefit'
(Putnam, 1993: 36). There is no universal formula in the computation of community quotient. A more structured attempt has been made in a massive community

survey that originated from the Saguaro Seminar at the John F. Kennedy School of Government of Harvard University.[3] The Saguaro Seminar selected a broadly diverse group of communities from interested applicants and conducted questionnaire surveys based on a number of issues in order to understand the following:

1 levels of informal socializing with others (neighbours, close friends, etc.);
2 levels of trust among residents and trust of government;
3 how diverse people's social networks are;
4 types of organization people are active in;
5 volunteering and philanthropy;
6 work-based social connectedness;
7 levels of family contact;
8 political engagement;
9 the use of the Internet among residents; and
10 religious participation.

Since the above list is based on the American community culture, certain adjustments are needed in order to suit the situation in Hong Kong for the purpose of this analysis to be outlined in this chapter.

The model

We follow the Harvard approach by identifying, as the first stage of analysis, major factors affecting residents' attachment to their housing community. This was conducted through general discussion/survey with the developers and property professionals in the field, and was followed by extensive review of the literature. Discussion/general survey with the developers/professionals is necessary as they are standing in the frontline of inputting design elements in housing community construction such that they should have more updated knowledge in the needs of the residents in the aspect of community attachment. We then analyzed the responses using the Analytic Hierarchy Process (AHP) and the multiple regression technique.

The AHP is a model for formulating a judgement on the relative weighting or ratio of each pair of objects within a system (Saaty, 1996). There is abundant literature on the technical aspects, as well as on the application of AHP in the real estate field (Armacost *et al.*, 1994; Ho *et al.*, 2005), so this chapter will not indulge in explaining the technical side of this analytical model.

The analysis

Residents living in public housing developments are not included as target respondents because they do not have the freedom to choose their accommodation up to a certain extent. The type of housing community that they are living in depends on the central allocation system of the HKSAR Government. This is in contrast to residents living in private housing developments who can have a free choice within their economic means.

Questionnaire surveys are carried out by means of street-level face-to-face interviews in three private housing estates in Hong Kong to examine the residents' willingness to stay in their housing community and their perception of the degree of different attributes contributing to their attachment to their housing community. A total of 267 qualified residents surveys are selected from more than one thousand interviewees who are chosen at random on the streets near the community as long as they identify themselves as residents in the respective community. This questionnaire is different from the discussion/survey applied on the developer/ professional group as this is the main data set for examination of residents' preferences. The target respondents are selected from the residents living in three major housing communities in Hong Kong, namely, Taikoo Shing[4], Whampoa Garden[5] and City One Shatin[6]. While there are 18 urban districts in Hong Kong, these three developments represent three major ones. In addition, these three communities are three of the larger ones in Hong Kong based on demand and number of residents. According to the annual Hong Kong Property Review issued by the Rating and Valuation Department of the HKSAR Government, these three communities appear to be three of the more popular housing communities in Hong Kong as transactions in these communities have been used in the calculation of the Private Domestic (Selected Popular Developments) Monthly Price Indices.[7]

It is expected that the residents living in these three private housing estates will provide significant and comprehensive indications for the examination of community attachment and housing choice in this chapter. It should also be noted that in the independent variables explained below, there is one variable called 'Type of Housing' representing the impact of private or public housing type. Although all respondents are residing at private housing communities, it is their view on whether private or public housing impacts on willingness to stay that matters.

The result

Weighting of attributes

As a first step, we analyze the relative weighting of the factors contributing to the bonding between residents within a community by means of the AHP procedure. As mentioned above, we carry out a pilot survey among professionals who have experience or views on this issue. A total of 82 questionnaires generated from the professional surveys are used to compute for the weighting analysis.

A hierarchical structure is developed to categorize the attributes using procedures similar to the Tree Diagram Approach. In this analysis, only two levels of hierarchy are considered. As indicated from previous literature, bonding among residents within a community can be reflected in several factors. Thus, the hierarchy structure is depicted in Figure 7.1.

This hierarchy structure is then used for the construction of the questionnaires. A nine-point scale is used in the questionnaires to allow the respondents to choose among 'equally preferred', 'slightly preferred,' 'moderately preferred,' 'strongly preferred,' or 'extremely preferred'. These preferences are for easier

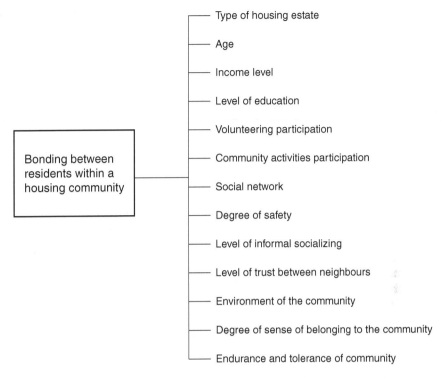

Figure 7.1 Hierarchy structure of residents' bonding within a housing community.

understanding of the respondents, while the actual input into the analysis is based on pairwise weights of 1 to 9.

The summation of each attribute weighting is equal to 1. The results are further summed up and then averaged to get the finalized respective weighting for each attribute in terms of residents' bonding within the community. The final weightings are listed in Table 7.1.

Among the category of factors affecting residents' bonding within the housing community, safety of the housing community (0.120579) is the most important, followed by the residents' sense of belonging towards their housing community (0.113711) and trust among neighbours (0.108132). The top three attributes are two or three times more important than community activities participation, volunteering participation, educational level, income level, and age distribution of the community. Meanwhile, the social network of residents (0.094974), environment (0.089), and endurance and tolerance of the community (0.078737) rank middle among all the 13 attributes. In conclusion, safety of the housing community and sense of belonging are the most significant factors affecting the bonding among residents within the housing community.

Table 7.1 Weights of residents' bonding within housing community attributes

	Final weighting	*Rank*
Types of housing estate	0.064342	8
Age of household	0.042947	13
Income level	0.047974	12
Level of education	0.052447	11
Volunteering participation	0.054737	10
Community activities participation	0.059132	9
Degree of safety	0.120579	1
Social network	0.094974	4
Level of trust among neighbours	0.108132	3
Level of informal socializing	0.073289	7
Environment of the community	0.089000	5
Degree of sense of belonging to the community	0.113711	2
Endurance and tolerance of the community	0.078737	6

Regression analysis on willingness to stay

Based on the examinations of the relative weightings of the variables, we analyzed the residents' willingness to stay in their respective housing communities (**WTS**) by regressing the 13 explanatory variables. These variables are elaborated as follows:

Types of housing estate (HOUSE)

Types of housing estates denote either private or public housing. It is believed that the type of housing estate, as well as the specific design, has a significant impact on residents' interaction with their neighbours, as well as their involvement in housing community, which in turn is the main component in determining the social capital of a community. Usually, public housing has a small range of designs depending on the phase of development to which a certain housing estate belongs. Private housing, however, has a much wider spectrum of designs.

Age (AGE)

Age refers to the average age of households within a particular housing community. Research suggests that the age of household members is correlated with residents' residential mobility. Younger residents tend to search continuously for a new home, for example due to more frequent change of job (Fuller, 2008), while the middle-aged prefer to stay in the same housing community where they have already settled down.

Income level (INCOM)

Income level refers to the average family monthly income of residents within a particular housing community. As we have discussed above, there is a correlation between the income level of residents and their mobility intentions.

Level of education (EDU)

Level of education represents the average educational level which the residents obtained within a particular housing community. It has been shown that higher education levels are associated with higher mobility rates. (For example, Checchi *et al.*, 1999 and Yankow, 2003.)

Volunteering participation (VP)

Volunteering participation refers to the frequency of volunteering activities in which residents participate in their respective housing communities. Volunteering participation represents formal and informal involvement in the community by the residents. Residents doing volunteering work in their housing community are believed to be more involved in their community because the frequency of inter-action with neighbours is increased. As a result, the linkage of people in the community is stronger, and a high level of social capital is produced.

Community services participation (CSP)

Community services participation refers to the frequency of participating in community services, in particular, the management of the community. Participation in community activities can be considered as informal or formal involvement in the community. Most of the private housing estates in Hong Kong have Incorporated Owners (IOs) set up under legislation as statutory body for owners to manage their buildings collaboratively on a self-help basis (Ho *et al.*, 2006). Where the owners do not want a statutory body of building management, they can also form non-statutory mutual-aid committees or owners committees. In any case, the committee members are all owners of the estate, and the chairman is usually elected through voting among the members. Acting as a committee member is a kind of a formal commitment to the housing community. In addition, IOs or owners committees also hold leisure events, such as outings and annual dinner for the residents. Involvement in these events can enhance interaction with neighbours in the community.

Degree of safety (SAFE)

The degree of safety is related to the frequency of victimization and reported crime occurrence. It also relates to the intrinsic perception towards safety by the residents. Thus, a high degree of victimization corresponds to a low degree of safety.

Social network (SN)

The social network of residents relates to the level of acquaintance among neighbours. A larger social network will enhance residents' perception of the sense of community as most people tend to know each other in the community.

Photo 7.1 One of the few low-density housing communities in Hong Kong that provides a nice environment for interactive social-networking among residents.

This is because the more neighbours one knows, the higher is one's perception of support to be gained in the community. Residents with a larger social network in the housing community tend to be more involved in community activities.

Level of trust among neighbours (TRUST)

The level of trust among neighbours is a perceived value. This can be indicated by whether the residents are willing to rely on their neighbours for help. The level of trust on neighbours can be increased by greater involvement in formal and informal activities within the housing community.

Level of informal socializing (IS)

The level of informal socializing is the measurement of the frequency of informal socializing with one's neighbours. Informal socializing includes activities such as home visits and leisure talk with neighbours. Therefore, the level of informal socializing of residents is regarded as one of the explanatory variables for their willingness to stay in their housing community.

Environment of the community (ENV)

The environment of the community refers to the physical environment surrounding the private housing estate. A good neighbourhood outlook enhances the positive sentiments of residents towards their housing community. This further acts as a 'pull' factor in accumulating the sense of neighbourhood.

Sense of belonging to the community (SOBC)

Sense of belonging to the community indicates the degree to which residents identify themselves as part of the immediate larger housing community. In an abstract perspective, the degree of the sense of belonging to the housing community can be reflected by the willingness and likelihood of residents to stay in their respective communities during holidays. Residents who are more likely to stay in their housing community during holidays may do so because of greater satisfaction (and comfort) they can seek in their own community on a non-working day.

Endurance and tolerance of the community (ETC)

Endurance and tolerance of the community refers to the willingness of residents to accept different ethnic groups or people of different backgrounds in their housing community.

An ordered Probit Regression model is employed to obtain the results because the data used for both dependent and independent variables were of ordinal, rating or categorized nature. Again, since this book is not about the technical aspect of research, details of Probit Analysis can be found from any search on the topic by a variety of authors (Mckelvey and Zavoina, 1975; Pelletiere and Reinert, 2004).

Variables are quantified in accordance with their ranking obtained in the AHP analysis. From the above, we specify the model specification as follows:

$$WTS = \alpha + \beta_1 HOUSE + \beta_2 AGE + \beta_3 INCOM + \beta_4 EDU + \beta_5 VP + \beta_6 CAP + \beta_7 SAFE + \beta_8 SN + \beta_9 TRUST + \beta_{10} IS + \beta_{11} ENV + \beta_{12} SOBC + \beta_{13} ETC + \varepsilon$$

where β_1, β_2, β_3, β_4, β_5, β_6, β_7, β_8, β_9, β_{10}, β_{11}, β_{12}, and β_{13} are the partial regression coefficients, whereas ε is the stochastic error term.

A simplified version of the regression analysis result is shown in Table 7.2.

From the probit analysis, we find that Degree of safety (SAFE) is statistically significant to the residents' neighbourhood attachment determination. It has a partial coefficient of 0.2398, which is the second largest absolute value of the partial coefficient among the 13 explanatory variables. This implies that when residents make decisions on moving, the degree of safety is a prime concern. A high degree of safety in the original community acts as a 'pull' factor deferring residents' decision to move out of the existing community, and vice versa.

Table 7.2 Summary of regression analysis results

Variable	Abbreviation	Absolute value of partial coefficient	Expected sign of partial coefficient	Actual sign of partial coefficient
Dependent variable				
Residents' willingness to stay in their housing community	WTS	N.A.	N.A.	N.A.
Independent variables				
Significant variables				
Safety of the community	SAFE	0.2398	+	+
Sense of belonging to the community	SOBC	0.2612	+	+
Insignificant variables				
Types of housing estate	HOUSE	0.1015	+	+
Age	AGE	0.1018	+	−
Income level	INCOM	0.0829	−	+
Level of education	EDU	0.0266	−	−
Volunteering participation	VP	0.0329	+	+
Community activities participation	CAP	0.0501	+	+
Social network	SN	0.0548	+	+
Level of trust among neighbours	TRUST	0.0859	+	+
Level of informal socializing	IS	0.0020	+	+
Environment of the community	ENV	0.0725	+	+
Endurance and tolerance of the community	ETC	0.0888	+	+

Sense of belonging to the community (SOBC) is also shown to be statistically significant with a partial regression coefficient of 0.2612. Among all the explanatory variables, sense of belonging can be said to be the most significant factor, having the largest absolute value of 0.2612 in its partial coefficient. Its absolute value is even 9 per cent higher than that of (SAFE). This implies that residents' being able to connect themselves to their own community produces a strong pull factor for them to stay with their respective housing communities.

The positive sign of its partial regression coefficient confirms that a high degree of sense of belonging reflects a higher likelihood of staying within the housing community, and thus a higher degree of attachment to the community. This is in relation to one's cognitions of satisfaction and expectations of stability in their housing community. For Hong Kong residents, if they are satisfied with their living environment and are gaining enough stability from their housing community, they tend not to move out easily. This is possibly a kind of psychological satisfaction among residents. The results suggest that in Hong Kong, among the three communities we have tested, the degree of sense of belonging of residents in a housing community has the greatest impact on their housing movement decision.

Chapter summary

We set out the criteria for examining the extent to which residents' attachment towards their housing community affects their willingness to stay. We borrowed and adapted the conceptual framework of Community Quotient (CQ) to review a set of factors believed to be instrumental in affecting the level of community attachment in Hong Kong. We did not attempt to compile the Community Quotient for Hong Kong because the original questionnaire adopted in the U.S. needed to be substantially amended to reflect socio-cultural differences. In addition, this may distort the outcome as far as the compilation of CQ is concerned. While this remains an interesting topic to be explored in Hong Kong, we concentrated on the examination of various factors that are likely to impact on residents' housing choice.

From the AHP analysis, we find the relative importance of the factors believed to be instrumental in affecting the level of community attachment in Hong Kong. Apart from financial considerations, we find two significant variables which have an impact on residents' attachment to their community. These include the degree of safety of the community and the sense of belonging. The findings from the empirical results have three major implications. First, the safety factor of the housing community determines residents' attachment to stay in the community to a large extent. Safety is a function of both real fear (generated by actual crime publicized in the community or personal experiences) and psychological fear (generated by residents' perception of their neighbours and the physical layout of their neighbourhood). This explains why gated communities are gaining popularity, because they allow for exclusiveness. This has further ramifications on the issue of community governance.

Second, sense of belonging affects residents' willingness to stay to the largest extent. This is in relation to the cognitive and psychological satisfaction and stability towards the residents' living environment. This implies that people do have their perception of what their own community stands for and how they want to be associated with it. It further implies that the management of space within the community is very important in enhancing the sense of belonging. By 'management of space', we mean the opportunities given to residents to use common areas such as clubhouse, garden, playground, or just open space. The findings in this analysis echo with our discussion above in Chapter 4. With an ideal physical design of the residential community, an effective and more human approach in space management provides a platform that effects the interaction among actors of the community. Residents need to be provided with a proper platform in the community to interact with each other so that they can get to experience a common feeling of being part of the larger family within the community. In compact urban areas such as Hong Kong where most of the housing structures are high-rise apartments, this is especially important.

Notes

1 This chapter is adapted from the paper by the author published in the academic journal *Property Management*. Full reference of the paper is Li, L. (2009) 'Community attachment and housing choice in Hong Kong', *Property Management*, 27 (1): 42–57. DOI: <http://dx.doi.org/10.1108/02637470910932665>. The author would like to thank Emerald Group Publishing Limited for granting the permission to reproduce the adapted version of this paper.
2 There are currently 18 District Councils in Hong Kong. These 18 District Councils are further divided into constituency areas. Each of these constituency areas is regarded by the government as a community system which has different domestic household subsystems interacting together.
3 John F. Kennedy School of Government, Harvard University, 2001. The Social Capital Community Benchmark Survey, [internet]. Community Foundation: Silicon Valley (Published 2001). Online. Available: <http://www.cfsv.org/communitysurvey/faqs.html>.
4 For basic information about Tai Koo Shing, please check <http://www.answers.com/main/ntquery;jsessionid=1r9g5pgmk3fyq?method=4&dsid=2222&dekey=Taikoo+Shing&curtab=2222_1&sbid=lc02b&linktext=Taikoo%20Shing>.
5 For basic information about Whampoa Garden, please check <http://www.answers.com/topic/whampoa-garden-1?method=8>.
6 For basic information about City One Shatin, please check <http://www.answers.com/City%20One%20Shatin>.
7 Rating and Valuation Department, HKSAR Government (2007), Hong Kong: R&V Dept. Online. Available: <http://www.rvd.gov.hk/en/publications/pro-review.htm> (accessed 20 December 2007).

8 Conclusion

Can real estate research
have a 'soft' side?

L.H. Li

I cannot emphasize enough that conventional real estate research that focuses on investment analysis and pricing models has a very important academic and practical role in our society. This book is by no means posing as a ground-breaking attempt to propose new research ideas in the real estate field. This is beyond doubt. However, this does not mean that we should be blinkered by this role when it comes to the understanding of how our urban built environment, which is about land and buildings, impacts our daily life (apart from wealth accumulation). The core objective of this book is to try to argue that real estate as a research theme and academic subject should not be merely constrained to being about business studies. The scope for a real estate angle in other aspects in our society is much wider than this. The examples outlined in the previous chapters have been well-recognized in the other disciplines as important research areas, though few researchers would associate them with 'real estate', as if stepping over this line will make the arguments more blurred.

I explained in the first chapter that if real estate is defined simply as buildings and land, this definition allows us to be more creative in relating real estate to other sectors of our society. This avoids real estate research being confined narrowly to just investment and business analyses. This also helps bridging real estate research with other related disciplines, in addition to investment and business studies. Real estate research does not have to be solely about real estate development or real estate investment, although without doubt these are important aspects of real estate studies, so that our society will be able to see that real estate is in fact an integral part of our life and to a greater extent more than most people (including non-property owners) realize.

We have seen in the various chapters in this book that real estate studies can be applied to the examination of the impacts on children and senior citizens. If these impacts are recognized as important, there will be implications on housing choice by the individuals, housing design by the developers and housing policy by the government. I remember presenting a paper on how the built environment impacts on children to the students and teaching staff in a faulty of transport and civil engineering nature in another university and, after the seminar, a lot of teaching staff approached me for a copy of the paper. They all told me that they never thought of that connection and, being a parent, they really wanted to know how to pick a better environment for their children's benefit. However, in responding to their new-found zealous interest in this aspect, I warned them that there is no golden rule or formula in improving child development just by adjusting the home environment, otherwise I would be working as a CEO for a major developer by now! The built environment is a very large set of intertwined variables and real estate, as well as other sectors, is only part of the system. A friend once told me that she read a paper which examined the reasons for behavioural problems of some younger children living in high-rise apartment buildings (and unfortunately we cannot find that paper to get the full reference!). One phenomenon is the apparent stronger tendency for younger children living on higher floors to have behavioural problems. One of the explanations given by the paper is the design of the elevator in the building, as the push buttons for all the floors are arranged in an order such that the lower floors (such as 1, 2, 3) are near the bottom of the panel, whereas the buttons for the top floors are on the top of the panel. Consequently, shorter and younger children who live on the top floors may not be allowed to go out to play with their peers for fear that they could not come home as they cannot press the button for their floor! A real estate solution to this is to provide a side panel inside the elevator, which is a simple design and facilities management for the community.

We have also seen in Chapter 7 that a lot of homebuyers tend to put safety as their priority when choosing a housing community. A passive real estate solution to this is the development of gated communities. Studies have shown this is not desirable for community culture development. A proactive real estate response to this desire for a safe environment is the realization of the benefits of mixed-use land development so that the community will also have the presence of people around any time of the day. This creates a natural neighbourhood watch system for the community.

What we have discussed and illustrated in the previous chapters are but a few examples of how one can relate the study of real estate to a much broader spectrum of research topics. There are indeed many more opportunities and possibilities for the understanding of our society when we expand the view to accept that we do live, work, play and age in a real estate environment. Such real estate environment transcends mere calculations of monetary gains and returns and therefore should appeal to an audience larger than just property owners, investors and developers. This is not all an epiphany. More likely, the importance of the 'soft' side of real estate in most mature urban societies including Hong Kong is very often overshadowed by the polarized sentiment towards real estate as a means of wealth accumulation between the 'haves' and 'have-nots'. Real estate has long been translated in money terms only without qualifications, and it is high time we did it justice!

I also need to emphasize that by looking at the other side of real estate research, it does not mean that there is a whole new set of analytical models or framework. We have seen in the previous chapters that the analytical/statistical framework of examining the impact of housing environment on children or senior citizens is more or less the same as an ordinary real estate investment analysis. It is just the change of focus that makes real estate research more interesting and less investment-oriented. Expanding the view of real estate research is not the same as limiting the conventional well-focused angle on investment analysis. On the contrary, it helps to expand the credibility of real estate research enormously. I have in the past few years presented various topics on real estate and child development to different audience groups, including UNICEF (Hong Kong) and the Rotary Club, and in all of these events, the audience commented that they were not aware that there could be a real estate angle in such a research topic. If real estate research is entirely insulated from other social aspects and activities and strictly defined as business and investment studies, such audience groups will remain indifferent towards the importance of real estate research and the gap between those who are working in the real estate industry, including researchers, and those who are not, will remain wide.

So where do we go from here? It is not the intention of this book to advocate a paradigm shift in real estate research. What is hoped to be achieved from this book is the understanding that real estate research is not a stand-alone subject, but a multi-disciplinary field in which there are uncharted waters waiting to be explored. Education research can have a real estate angle as school location, school design and impact of school on the neighbourhood rest on decisions of utilization of buildings and land. The same therefore can also be applied to health care research, social security as well as rural environment protection.

Since real estate research is a multi-disciplinary research field, the implications of such research are also multi-disciplinary in nature. For example, if real estate is applied to community studies to examine what land use environment may benefit the local neighbourhood, a possible result may be for the government to advocate that developers build a more vibrant community rather than just apartment buildings/structures. This may have further implications on government land sale policies as this means larger sites rather than smaller sites should be put to the market, other things being equal. This may also in turn affect the government's infrastructure and provision of public services in the neighbourhood. However, there may also be potential accusation from society of the government's nepotism towards larger developers as they are financially more capable of outbidding smaller developers for bigger sites. Similarly, if it could be proved that mixed-use neighbourhoods tend to be beneficial to the residents, there will be a need for a review of land use and zoning policies. (For example, the town of Emeryville near San Francisco was an industrial suburb in slow decline. Emeryville made the transition from smokestack industry to vibrant mixed-use by scrapping antiquated zoning conventions and obsolete factory buildings, many of which were likely to be selected for demolition but were converted into high-tech commercial and live/work spaces.) This may in turn also affect provision of public services in the neighbourhood, as well as concerns over fire and traffic hazards.

This list could go on forever, but the point remains the same. We live in a network of systems. No one aspect of our lives can or should be singled out and judged on its own merits. This does not only apply to real estate research, though this is the focus of this book. I hope this book has illustrated this point and next time when I go to a conference not in the conventional real estate theme of business and investment nature, I will not have to explain why I am the black sheep!

Bibliography

Adair, A., Berry, J. and McGreal, S. (1996) 'Valuation of residential property: analysis of participant behavior', *Journal of Property Valuation and Investment*, 14 (1): 20–35.

Aged & Community Services Australia (2004) 'Older people and aged care in rural, regional and remote Australia', discussion paper prepared by the Aged & Community Services Australia.

Armacost, R.L., Componation, P.J., Mullens, M.A. and Swart, W.W. (1994) 'An AHP framework for prioritizing customer requirements in QFD: an industrialized housing application', *IIE Transactions*, 26 (4): 72–9.

Aroul, R.R. (2009) 'Going green – impact on residential property values', (Order No. 1467938, The University of Texas at Arlington), unpublished PhD thesis, The University of Texas at Arlington. Online. Available: <http://search.proquest.com/docvi ew/305175096?accountid=14548>. (305175096).

Arthurson, K. (2012) *Social Mix and the City: challenging the mixed communities consensus in housing and urban planning policies*. Collingwood, Victoria: CSIRO Publishing.

Baba, Y. and Austin, D.M. (1989) 'Neighbourhood environmental satisfaction, victimization and social participation as determinants of perceived neighbourhood safety', *Environment and Behavior*, 21 (6): 763.

Baldassare, M., Rosenfield, S. and Rook, K. (1984) 'The types of social relations predicting elderly well-being', *Research on Aging*, 6 (4): 549–59. Online. Available: <http://search.proquest.com/docview/61077509?accountid=14548>.

Ball, M. (1998) 'Institutions in British property research: a review', *Urban Studies*, 35: 1501–17.

Beggs, J.J., Hurlbert, J.S. and Haines, V.A. (1996) 'Community attachment in a rural setting: a refinement and empirical test of the Systemic Model', *Rural Sociology*, 61: 407–26.

Berry, J. (2001) 'Behavioral Economics: where does it fit in?', *Consulting to Management*, 12 (3): 49–52.

Blakeley, Kim (1994) 'Parents' conceptions of social dangers to children in the urban environment', *Children's Environments*, 11: 16–25.

Bogdonoff, M.D., Hughes, S.L., Weissert, W.G. and Paulsen, E. (eds) (1991) *The Living at Home Program: innovations in service access and case management*. New York: Springer Publishing Co.

Bourassa, S.C. and Hoesli, M. (2010) 'Why do the swiss rent?', *Journal of Real Estate Finance and Economics*, 40 (3): 286–309.

Brehm, Joan M., Eisenhauer, Brian W. and Krannich, Richard S. (2004) 'Dimensions of community attachment and their relationship to well-being in the amenity-rich rural west', *Rural Sociology*, 69 (3): 405–29.

Brink, S. (1997) *Housing Older People: an international perspective.* New Brunswick, N.J.: Transaction Publishers.

Brooks-Gunn, J., Duncan, G.J. and Aber, J.L. (1997) *Neighbourhood Poverty: context and consequences for children.* New York: Russell Sage Foundation.

Bryant, Christopher R. (1999) 'Community change in context', in Pierce, John T. and Dale, Ann (eds) *Communities, Development, and Sustainability across Canada.* Vancouver: UBC Press.

Buckey, J., Schneider, M. and Shang, Y. (2004) *LAUSD School Facilities and Academic Performance.* Los Angeles, Unified School Districts. Online. Available: <http://www.ncef.org/pubs/LAUSD%20Report.pdf>.

Camerer, Colin F. and Loewenstein, George (2004) 'Behavioral Economics: past, present and future', in Camerer, Loewenstein and Rabin (eds) (2004) *Advances in Behavioral Economics.* New York: Princeton University Press.

Carter, William H., Schill, Michael H. and Wachter, Susan M. (1997) 'Polarisation, public housing and racial minorities in US cities', *Urban Studies*, 35: 1889–911.

Casey, R., Coward, S., Allen, C. and Powell, R. (2007) 'On the planned environment and neighbourhood life: evidence from mixed-tenure housing developments twenty years on', *Town Planning Review*, 78 (3).

Census and Statistics Department (2008) *Thematic Report: Older Persons for 2006 By-census.*, Hong Kong.

Checchi, Daniele, Ichino, Andrea and Rustichini, Aldo (1999) 'More equal but less mobile? Education financing and intergenerational mobility in Italy and in the US', *Journal of Public Economics*, Amsterdam: 74 (3): 351–93.

Chui, E. (2000) 'Boom the city, doom the elderly: housing problems of elderly affected by urban redevelopment in Hong Kong', *Hallym International Journal of Aging*, 2 (2), 119–34. Online. Available: <http://search.proquest.com/docview/60422907?accountid=14548>.

Coleman, J.S. (1990) *Foundations of Social Theory.* Cambridge, MA: Harvard University Press.

Coley, Rebekah Levine, Kuo, Frances E. and Sullivan, William C. (1997) 'Where does community grow? The social context created by nature in urban public housing', *Environment and Behavior*, 29 (4): 468–94.

Conway, S. (2004) 'Stigma-induced property value diminution from nuclear waste transportation', (Order No. 3135242, Arizona State University), unpublished PhD thesis, Arizona State University. Online. Available: <http://search.proquest.com/docview/305211715?accountid=14548>. (305211715).

Currie, A. and Yelowitz, A. (2000) 'Are public housing projects good for kids?', *Journal of Public Economics*, 75: 99–124.

David, R.P. and Alfred, C.M. (2002) *Ageing and Long-term Care: national policies in the Asia-Pacific.* Hong Kong: ISEAS/IDRC/TRF.

Davies, Wayne K.D. and Herbert, David T. (1993) *Communities within Cities; an urban social geography.* London: Belhaven Press.

Davis-Kean, P.E. (2005) 'The influence of parent education and family income on child achievement: the indirect role of parental expectations and the home environment', *Journal of Family Psychology*, 19: 294–304.

Davison, B., Kendig, H., Stephens, F. and Merrill, V. (1993) *It's My Place: older people talk about their home.* Canberra: Australian Government Publishing Service.

DeSalvo, J. (1974) 'Neighbourhood upgrading effects of middle income housing projects in New York City', *Journal of Urban Economics*, 1: 269–77.

Diaz III, J. (1999) 'The first decade of behavioral research in the discipline of property', *Journal of Property Investment and Finance*, 17: 326–30.

Diaz III, J. and Hansz, J.A. (2001) 'The use of reference points in valuation judgement', *Journal of Property Research*, 18: 141–8.

Diaz III, J. and Wolverton, M.L. (1998) 'A longitudinal examination of the Appraisal Smoothing Hypothesis', *Real Estate Economics*, 26 (2): 349–58.

Dickson, G. (2002) 'The IT evolution: attitudinal audit of commercial real estate industry and information technology', (Order No. MQ77383, University of Calgary, Canada), unpublished PhD thesis, University of Calgary. Online. Available: <http://search.proquest.com/docview/304806694?accountid=14548>. (304806694).

Dudek, M. (2000) *Architecture of Schools: the new learning environments*. Oxford: Architectural Press.

Duncan, G. and Raudenbush, S. (1999) 'Assessing the effects of context in studies of child and youth development', *Educational Psychology*, 34 (1): 29–41.

Dunegan, K. (2010) 'GPA and attribute framing effects: Are better students more sensitive or more susceptible?', *Journal of Education for Business*, 85 (4): 239–47. Online. Available: <http://search.proquest.com/docview/745602426?accountid=14548>.

Dunse, N., Jones, C. and White, M. (2010) 'Valuation accuracy and spatial variations in the efficiency of the property market', *Journal of European Real Estate Research*, 3 (1): 24–45.

Durbin, J. and Watson, G.S. (1951) 'Testing for serial correlation in least squares regression, II', *Biometrika*, 38: 159–78.

Edwards, A.D. and Jones, D.G. (1976) *Community and Community Development*, Netherlands: Mouton & Co.

Eekelaar, J. (1986) 'The emergence of children's rights', *Oxford Journal of Legal Studies*, 6: 161–82.

Evans, G.W. (2006) 'Child development and the physical environment', *Annual Review of Psychology*, 57: 423–51.

Evans, G.W., Kantrowitz, E. and Eshelman, P. (2002) 'Housing quality and psychological well-being among the elderly population', *The Journal of Gerontology*, 57 (4): 381–3.

Evans, G.W., Saegert, S. and Harris, R. (2001) 'Residential density and psychological health among children in low-income families', *Environment and Behavior*, 33 (2): 165–80.

Evans, G.W., Wells, N.M. and Moch, A. (2003) 'Housing and mental health: a review of the evidence and a methodological and conceptual critique', *The Journal of Social Issues*, 59: 475.

Farley, J.E. (1982) ' Has public housing gotten a bum rap? The incidence of crime in St. Louis public housing developments', *Environment and Behavior*, 14: 445–7.

Feinstein, L. and Symons, J. (1999) 'Attainment in secondary school', *Oxford Economic Papers*, 51: 300–21.

Fredland, D.R. (1974) *Residential Mobility and Home Purchase*. United States: Lexington Books.

Freeman, L. and Botein, H. (2002) 'Subsidized housing and neighbourhood impacts: a theoretical discussion and review of the evidence', *Journal of Planning Literature*, 16 (3): 359–78.

Fried, M. (1984) 'The structure and significance of community satisfaction', *Population and Environment*, 7 (2): 61–86.

Fu, Y. and Ng, L.K. (2001) 'Market efficiency and return statistics: evidence from real estate and stock markets using a present-value approach', *Real Estate Economics*, 29 (2): 227–50.

Fujimoto, H. and Park, E.S. (2010) 'Framing effects and gender differences in voluntary public goods provision experiments', *The Journal of Socio-Economics*, 39: 455–7.

Fuller, S. (2008) 'Job mobility and wage trajectories for men and women in the United States', *American Sociological Review*, Albany, 73 (1): 158–83.

Galle, O.R., Gove, W.R. and McPherson, J.M. (1972) 'Population density and pathology: what are the relations for man?' *Science, New Series*, 176 (4030): 23–30.

Gallimore, P. and Wolverton, M. (1997) 'Price-knowledge-induced bias: a cross-cultural comparison', *Journal of Property Valuation & Investment*, 15 (3): 261–73. Online. Available: <http://search.proquest.com/docview/212963533?accountid=14548>.

Genesove, David and Mayer, Christopher (2004) 'Loss-aversion and seller behavior: evidence from the housing market', in Camerer, Loewenstein and Rabin (eds) (2004) *Advances in Behavioral Economics*. New York: Princeton University Press.

Gerstle, M. (2008) 'Tree preservation and its impact on residential development and real estate value', (Order No. 1456534, The University of Texas at Arlington), unpublished PhD thesis, The University of Texas at Arlington. Online. Available: <http://search.proquest.com/docview/194046350?accountid=14548>. (194046350).

Gibler, K.M. and Nelson, S.L. (2003) 'Consumer behavior applications to real estate education', *Journal of Real Estate Practice and Education*, 6.

Gifford, R. and Lacombe, C.C. (2006) 'Housing quality and children's socioemotional health', *Journal of Housing and the Built Environment*, 21: 177.

Goodman, A.M. and Hankin, J.R. (1984) 'Elderly Jews and happiness with locale', *Population and Environment*, 7 (2): 87–102.

Goudy, W.J. (1990) 'Community attachment in rural region', *Rural Sociology*, 55: 178–98.

Guest, A.M. and Lee, B.A. (1983) 'Sentiment and evaluation as ecological variables', *Sociological Perspectives*, 26 (2): 158–84.

Gump, P.V. (1987) 'School and classroom environments', in Stokols, D. and Altman, I. (eds) *Handbook of Environmental Psychology.*, New York: Wiley.

Gurney, C. and Means, R. (1993) 'The meaning of home in later life', in S. Arber and M. Evandrou (eds) *Aging, Independence and the Life Course*. London: Jessica Kingsley.

Guster, L. (2002) *Housing Options for Older People: a discussion paper*. The Older Person's Housing Advisory Network (OPHAN) and Shelter SA., 4.

Gutenschwager, Gerald (1995) 'Ekistic environment and influences on the child', *Ekistics*, 62 (373–5): 289–93.

Harris, R.J. (2009) *A Cognitive Psychology of Mass Communication*, Mahwah, NJ: L. Erlbaum Associates.

Hart, R.A. (1997) *Children's Participation: the theory and practice of involving young citizens in community development and environmental care*. London: Earthscan.

Havard, Timothy M. (2001) 'An experimental evaluation of the effect of data presentation on heuristic bias in commercial valuation', *Journal of Property Research*, 18 (1): 51–67, E. and F.N. Spon.

Hawkins, R.P., Pingree, S. and Adler, I. (1987) 'Searching for cognitive processes in the cultivation effect: adult and adolescent samples in the United States and Australia', *Human Communication Research*, 13: 553–77.

Heumann, L.F. and Boldy, D.P. (1993) *Aging in Place with Dignity – international solutions relating to the low-income and frail elderly*. Westport, CT: Praeger.

Heywood, F., Oldman, C. and Means, R. (2001) *Housing and Home in Later Life*. Buckingham: Open University Press.

Hillier, J., Fisher, C. and Tonts, M. (2002) *Rural Housing Regional Development and Policy Integration: An Evaluation of Alternative Policy Responses to Regional Disadvantage*, AHURI, February 2002.

Ho, D., Newell, G. and Walker, A. (2005) 'The importance of property-specific attributes in assessing CBD office building quality', *Journal of Property Investment & Finance*, 23 (5): 424–44.

Ho, D., Yung, Y., Wong, S.K. and Cheung, A.K.C. (2006) 'Effects of building management regimes of private apartment buildings in Hong Kong', *Property Management*, Bradford, 24 (3): 309.

Hong Kong Housing Society (2004) *Comprehensive Study on the Housing Needs of the Elderly in Hong Kong: executive summary: quality with choice.*

Hong Kong Polytechnic University, School of Design, Research Group on Urban Space and Culture (2000) *Project on Newly Designed Living Environment for the Elderly: Research Report*. Hong Kong: Hong Kong Polytechnic University.

Hyde, J.S. (2005) 'The gender similarities hypothesis', *American Psychologist*, 60 (6): 581–92.

Jacobs, Jane (1964) *The Death and Life of Great American Cities*. Harmondsworth: Penguin Books.

Jamieson, K.H. and Campbell, K.K. (1992) *The Interplay of Influence: news, advertising, politics, and the mass media*. Belmont, CA: Wadsworth.

Jin, C. (2009) 'The impact of local media pessimism on residential real estate markets', Doctor of Philosophy thesis, Georgia State University.

Jin, Jang C. and Yu, Eden S.H. (2011) 'World ranking of real estate research: recent changes in school competitiveness and research institutions', *Journal of Real Estate Finance and Economics*, 42: 229–46.

Joseph, M. (2010) 'Creating mixed-income developments in Chicago: developer and service provider perspectives', *Housing Policy Debate*, 20 (1): 91–118, DOI: 10.1080/10511481003599894.

Joseph, M. and Chaskin, R. (2010) 'Living in a mixed-income development: resident perceptions of the benefits and disadvantages of two developments in Chicago', *Urban Studies*, 1: 20, DOI: 10.1177/0042098009357959.

Karsada, J.D. and Janowitz, M. (1974) 'Community attachment in mass society', *American Sociological Review*, 39: 328–39.

Kashian, R. and Rockwell, Steven J. (2013) 'Town and gown: the negative externality of a university on housing prices', *Journal of Real Estate Practice and Education*, 16 (1): 1–12.

Katz, P. (1994) *The New Urbanism: toward an architecture of community*. New York: McGraw Hill.

Kees, J. (2011) 'Advertising framing effects and consideration of future consequences', *The Journal of Consumer Affairs*, 45: 7–32.

Kelly, Eric D. and Becker, Barbara (2000) *Community Planning: an introduction to the comprehensive plan*. Washington, D.C: Island Press.

Kichen, J. and Roche, J. (1987) 'Life care resident preferences: a survey of the decision-making process to enter a CCRC', in R.D. Chellis and P.J. Grayson (eds) *Life Care: a long-term solution?*, 49–60, Lexington, MA: Lexington.

Knobloch-Westerwick, S. and Alter, S. (2006) 'Mood adjustment to social situations through mass media use: how men ruminate and women dissipate angry moods', *Human Communication Research*, 32: 58–73.

Lang, A. and Shapiro, M.A. (1991) 'Making television reality: unconscious processes in the construction of social reality', *Communication Research*, 18: 685–705.

Lasch, C. (1995) *The Revolt of the Elites and the Betrayal of Democracy*. New York: W.W. Norton.

Lemasters, L.K. (1997) 'A synthesis of studies pertaining to facilities, student achievement, and student behavior', unpublished Ed. D. thesis, Virginia Polytechnic and State University.

Levy, D. and Schuck, E. (1999) 'The influence of clients on valuations', *Journal of Property Investment & Finance*, 17 (4): 380. Online. Available: <http://search.proquest.com/docview/212952952?accountid=14548>.

Li, L.H. (2005) 'Value of stigma – impact of social housing on private neighbourhood', *The Appraisal Journal*, Summer 2005,Vol. LXXIII, No. 3: 305–17.

Li, L.H. (2009) 'Built environment and children's academic performance – a Hong Kong perspective', *Habitat International*, 33: 45–51.

Li, L.H. and Siu, A. (2001) 'Privatising management services in subsidised housing in Hong Kong', *Property Management*, 19:1.

Lozza, E., Carrera, S. and Bosio, A.C. (2010) 'Perceptions and outcomes of a fiscal bonus: framing effects on evaluations and sage intentions', *Journal of Economic Psychology*, 31: 400–4.

Lynch, Kevin (1977) *Growing Up in Cities*. London: MIT Press.

Malone, K. (2002) 'Exposing intolerance and exclusion and building communities of difference', keynote address, Youth Coalition Symposium 'Youth and Public Space', Opening of Youth Week, National Museum, Canberra, 8 April 2002.

Malone, K. and Tranter, P.J. (2003) 'School grounds as sites for learning: making the most of environmental opportunities', *Environmental Education Research*, 9: 283–303.

MaRous, Michael S. (1996) 'Low-income housing in our backyards: what happens to residential property values?', *The Appraisal Journal*, Jan 1996, 64 (1): 27–35.

Massey, Douglas (2001) 'The prodigal paradigm returns: ecology comes back to Sociology' in Booth, Alan and Crouter, Ann C. (2001) (eds) *Does It Take a Village? Community Effects on Children, Adolescents, and Families*. Mahwah, NJ: Lawrence Erlbaum Associates Publishers.

Maxwell, L.E. (2003) 'Home and school density effects on elementary school children: the role of spatial density', *Environment and Behavior*, 35 (4): 566–78.

Mckelvey, R.D. and Zavoina, W. (1975) 'A statistical model for the analysis of ordinal level dependent variables', *The Journal of Mathematical Sociology*, 4 (1): 103–20, DOI: 10.1080/0022250X.1975.9989847.

Mitchell, R.F. (1971) 'Some social implications of high density housing', *American Sociological Review*, 36: 18–29.

Moore, G.T. and Lackney, J.A. (1993) 'School design: crisis, educational performance and design applications', *Children's Environments*, 10: 99–112.

Mroczek, D.K. and Kolarz, C.M. (1998) 'The effect of age on positive and negative affect: a developmental perspective on happiness', *Journal of Personality and Social Psychology*, 75 (5): 1333–49.

Mueller, E.J. and Tighe, J.R. (2007) 'Making the case for affordable housing: connecting housing with health and education outcomes', *Journal of Planning Literature*, 21 (4): 371–85, DOI: <http://dx.doi.org/10.1177/0885412207299653>.

Nadel, L. (2003) *Encyclopedia of Cognitive Science*. London: Nature Publishing Group.

Nourse, Hugh O. (1963) 'The effect of public housing on property values in St. Louis', *Land Economics*, 39: 433–41.

O'Neill, D.J. and Oates, A.D. (2001) 'The impact of school facilities on student achievement, behavior, attendance, and teacher turnover rate in central Texas middle schools', *Educational Facility Planner*, 36: 14–22.

Ontario Ministry of Community and Social Services (1989) *Better Beginnings, Better Futures: an integrated model of primary prevention of emotional and behaviour problems*. Toronto: Queen's Printer.

Pastalan, L. (1970) 'Privacy as an expression of human territoriality', in Pastalan, L. and Carson, D. (eds) *Spatial Behavior of Older People*. Ann Arbor, MI: University of Michigan.

Pastalen, L.A. (1990) *Ageing in Place: the role of housing and social support*. New York: Haworth.

Pelletiere, D. and Reinert, K.A. (2004) 'Used automobile protection and trade: gravity and ordered probit analysis', *Empirical Economics*, 29 (4): 737–51.

Perla Jr. H. (2011) 'Explaining public support for the use of military force: the impact of reference point framing and prospective decision making', *International Organization*, 65: 139–67.

Pettersson, G. (1997) 'Crime and mixed use development', in Coupland, A. (ed.) *Reclaiming The City: mixed use development*. London: E & FN Spon.

Phillips, D.R., and Chan, A.C.M. (2002) *Ageing and Long-term Care: national policies in the Asia-Pacific*. Singapore: Institute of Southeast Asian Studies.

Phillips, L. (2000) 'Domestic violence and aging women', *Geriatric Nursing*, 21 (4): 188–95.

Porell, F.W. (1982) *Models of Intraurban Residential Relocation*. United States: Kluwer Nijhoff Publishing.

Putnam, R. (1993) 'The prosperous community; social capital and indirect effects in multilevel designs with latent variables', *The American Prospect*, Spring, 35–42.

Rabiega, W.A., Lin, TA-WIN and Robinson, L.M. (1984) 'The property value impacts of public housing projects in low and moderate density residential neighbourhoods', *Land Economics*, 60: 174–9.

Reese, S. D. (2007) 'The framing project: a bridging model for media research revisited', *Journal of Communication*, 57: 148–54.

Roof, K. and Oleru, N. (2008) 'Public health: Seattle and King County's push for the built environment', *Journal of Environmental Health*, 71: 24–7.

Rosenberg, G. (1970) *The Worker Grows Old*. San Francisco: Jossey-Bass.

Rossi, P.H. (1980) *Why Families Move*. New York: SAGE Publications, Inc.

Saaty, T.L. (1996) *The Analytic Hierarchy Process: planning, priority setting, resource allocation*, United States of America: University of Pittsburgh.

Saaty, T.L. and Niemira, M.P. (2006) 'A framework for making a better decision', *Research Review*, 13.

Samdal, O., Wold, B. and Bronis, M. (1999) 'Relationship between students' perceptions of school environment, their satisfaction with school and perceived academic achievement: an international study', *School Effectiveness and School Improvement*, 10: 296–320.

Sampson, R., Raudenbush, S. and Earls, F. (1997) 'Neighbourhood and violent crime: a multilevel study of collective efficacy', *Science*, 277: 918–24.

Sampson, Robert J. (2001) 'How do communities undergrid or undermine human development? Relevant contexts and social mechanisms', in Booth, Alan and Crouter, Ann C. (2001) (eds) *Does It Take a Village? Community Effects on Children, Adolescents, and Families*. Mahwah, NJ: Lawrence Erlbaum Associates Publishers.

Santiago, Anna M., Galster, George C. and Tatian, Peter (2001) 'Assessing the property value impacts of the dispersed housing subsidy program in Denver', *Journal of Policy Analysis and Management*, 20 (1): 65–88.

Scheufele, D.A. and Tewksbury, D. (2007) 'Framing, agenda setting, and priming: evolution of three media effects models', *Journal of Communication*, 57: 9–20.

Shapiro, M.A. (1991) 'Memory and decision processes in the construction of social reality', *Communication Research*, 18: 3–24.

Sidnell, J. (1995) 'Elicitations as a resource for organizing social and spatial location in an Indo-Guyanese Village', *Journal of Linguistic Anthropology*, 7 (2): 143–65.

Simpson, Brian (1997) 'Towards the participation of children and young people in urban planning and design', *Urban Studies*, 34 (5–6): 907–25.

Skeffington, A.M. (1969) *People and Planning: Report of the Committee on Public Participation in Planning*, (The Skeffington Report). London: HMSO.

Skogan, W.G. (1987) 'The impact of victimization on fear', *Crime and Delinquency*, New York, 33 (1): 135.

Small, Stephen and Supple, Andrew (2001) 'Communities as systems: is a community more than the sum of its parts?', in Booth, Alan and Crouter, Ann C. (2001) (eds) *Does It Take a Village? Community Effects on Children, Adolescents, and Families*. Mahwah, NJ: Lawrence Erlbaum Associates Publishers.

Smith, Vernon L. (2005) 'Behavioral economics research and the foundations of economics', *The Journal of Socio-Economics*, 34: 135–50.

Stokols, D. (1976) 'The experience of crowding in primary and secondary environments', *Environment and Behavior*, 8: 792–814.

Streib, F. Gordon, LaGreca, J. Anthony and Folts, E. William (1986) *Retirement Communities: People, Planning, Prospect, Housing an Ageing Society*. New York: Van Nostrand Reinhold Company Inc.

Streib, G. F., Folts, W. E. and Hilker, M. A. (1984) *Old Homes - New Families: shared living for the elderly*, New York: Columbia University Press.

Talen, E. (2008) *Design for Diversity: exploring socially mixed neighbourhoods*. New York: Routledge.

Tanner, C.K. (2000) 'The influence of school architecture on academic achievement', *Journal of Educational Administration*, 38: 309–30.

Theodori, G.L. (2000) 'Levels of analysis and conceptual clarification in community attachment and satisfaction literature: connection to community development', *Journal of Community Development Society*, 31: 35–58.

Torrell, G. (1990) 'Children's conception of large scale environments', *Goteborg Psychological Reports*, 20 (2).

Tversky, A. and Kahneman, D. (1974) 'Judgment under uncertainty: Heuristics and biases', *Science*, 185 (4157): 1124–31. Online. Available: <http://search.proquest.com/docview/615977357?accountid=14548>.

Vandegrift, D., Lockshiss, A. and Lahr, M. (2012) 'Town versus gown: the effect of a college on housing prices and the tax base', *Growth and Change*, 43: 304–34. doi: 10.1111/j.1468-2257.2012.00587.x

Valentine, Gill (1996) 'Children should be seen and not heard: the production and transgression of adults' public space', *Urban Geography*, 17 (3): 205–20.

Veenhoven, R. (2005) 'Is life getting better?: how long and happily do people live in modern society?', *European Psychologist*, 10 (4): 330–43, DOI: <http://dx.doi.org/10.1027/1016-9040.10.4.330>.

Veenhoven, R. *World Database of Happiness*, The Netherlands: Erasmus University Rotterdam. Online. Available: <http://worlddatabaseofhappiness.eur.nl> (assessed 2 January 2012).

de Vreese, C.H., Boomgaarden, H.G. and Semetko, H.A. (2011) '(In)direct framing effects: the effects of news media framing on public support for Turkish membership in the European Union', *Communication Research*, 38: 2.

Wedding, G. Christopher (2008) 'Understanding sustainability in real estate: a focus on measuring and communicating success in green building', unpublished PhD thesis, The University of North Carolina at Chapel Hill Environmental Sciences & Engineering.

Weinstein, C.S. (1979) 'The physical environment of the school: a review of the research', *Review of Educational Research*, 49: 577–610.

Wilensky, J. (2002) 'Analyzing the effects of the physical environment', *Human Ecology*, 30: 20–2.

Wilson, W.J. (1987) *The Truly Disadvantaged: the inner city, the underclass, and public policy*. Chicago, IL: University of Chicago Press.

Wireman, P. and Sebastian, A.G. (1986) 'Environmental consideration for housing sites for the elderly', in R.J. Newcomer, M.P. Lawton and T.O. Byerts (eds) *Housing an Aging Society: issues, alternatives, and policy*, 168–77. New York: Van Nostrand.

Wolverton, M. L. and Gallimore, P. (1999) 'A cross-cultural comparison of the appraisal profession', *The Appraisal Journal*, 67 (1): 47–56. Online. Available: <http://search.proquest.com/docview/199952311?accountid=14548>.

Woolley, Helen, Spencer, Christopher, Dunn, Jessica and Rowley, Gwyn (1999) 'The child as citizen: experiences of British town and city centres', *Journal of Urban Design*, 4, (3): 255–82.

Wright, P.A. and Kloos, B. (2007) 'Housing environment and mental health outcomes: a levels of analysis perspective', *The Journal of Environmental Psychology*, 27 (1): 79–89.

Wu, H., Wong, S.K., McKinnell, K., Reed, R. and Robinson, J. 'Commercial property markets and property cycles in Chinese cities', PRRES Conference, Sydney, January 2009.

Yankow, Jeffrey J. (2003) 'Migration, job change, and wage growth: a new perspective on the pecuniary return to geographic mobility', *Journal of Regional Science*, Heightstown, 43 (3): 483–516.

Yuen, Belinda and Yeh, Anthony, G.O. (eds) (2011) *High-Rise Building Living in Asian Cities*. Hong Kong: Springer.

Index

Page numbers in italic refer to tables/figures
Page numbers followed by 'n' refer to notes